THE BOXER REBELLION

The Boxer Rebellion

BY
CHRISTOPHER
MARTIN

ILLUSTRATED WITH PHOTOGRAPHS AND MAPS

ABELARD-SCHUMAN
London New York Toronto

Library of Congress Catalogue Card Number: 68-13241
Standard Book Number: 200.71542.9

Grateful acknowledgment is made to Rupert Hart-Davis Limited of London, publishers of *The Siege at Peking* by Peter Fleming, for permission to use several of the maps drawn for that book by K. C. Jordan. These maps appear on pages 27, 54, 120 and 133.

LONDON	NEW YORK	TORONTO
Abelard-Schuman Limited	Abelard-Schuman Limited	Abelard-Schuman Canada Limited
8 King St. WC2	257 Park Ave. S.	1680 Midland Ave.

An Intext Publisher

Printed in the United States of America

Books by Christopher Martin

THE BOXER REBELLION

THE RUSSO-JAPANESE WAR

Contents

Illustrations

Prefatory Note

Any book about so minor a patch in the desert of time as the Boxer Rebellion is likely to be greeted with a challenge as to the reason, if any, that such a book should be written, or a demand that the events be pointed up for the easy understanding of a reader concerned only with the present time. Yet even as this book was going to press the name of the Society of Righteous and Harmonious Fists was appearing in the pages of the daily newspapers and news magazines. The reason was that the anti-foreignism of the Chinese Communists in Peking had broken into violence against foreign diplomatic representatives in the summer of 1967, and journalists were comparing this outbreak with the Boxer Rebellion. So facts and events bring about the comparisons.

It will be said by some, as it has been said about other books of this sort, that it is an account of a war that nobody cares about. But as with the author's first book of this kind, *The Russo-Japanese War,* there is room for caring about such things in America, by those who wish to understand the events of the recent past and to seek clues to the future in Asia. Not all books about wars need to depend on derring-do and excitement; perhaps it is better to learn early in life that war is a dirty, deadly, dull, repetitive and stupid business, and there is no better way to learn than to be exposed to some of the repetitions that occur in every war in history. I have not tried to avoid these repetitions in this book, or in others, and although some readers have faulted me for sticking to the facts and keeping events in their true historical perspective, that is how it was. Let it be understood that this is a book about the Boxer Rebellion and its immediate antecedents. It is not a survey of Chinese history; not a personal history of the people who withstood the siege of Peking; not an analysis of the American position, or the British position or any other; and it is not written with perspective disjointed so as to bring forth the direct connections and references to the United States.

I might have dwelt at length on John Hay's Open Door Policy; I might have dwelt on the generosity of the United States in turning its part of the reparations over to the education of Chinese students in order to better Chinese-American relations; but these are not important parts of the Boxer Rebellion story and no wishing will make them so. In fact, Americans were included among the "hates" of the Boxers basically because of the large number of American missionaries in China, whereas the hatred of missionaries and Christianity in general was caused by the depredations of the European powers in matters of trade, commerce and ownership – matters in which the United States was very little involved.

PREFATORY NOTE

In the constant search to identify events in foreign lands with things American, we tend to oversimplify; the fact remains that there would have been a Boxer rebellion had there not been one American in China, and it would have come out the same way, except that the terms of settlement would probably have been slightly harsher, as I have indicated in this book. There is no way that I know to condense the thousands of years of Chinese history into sweetmeats for a jaded palate or to make this book serve as a text on Chinese history, Chinese relations with the Western world or any other set of facts than those of the Boxer Rebellion itself.

There is a tendency among Americans to oversimplify history so that young people may swallow it in great gulps and pretend that they have digested it, but there is also a place in historical writing for brief surveys, aimed at young people and adults who want a general understanding of a specific subject. One might write a several-volume study of the Boxer Rebellion; dozens of its aspects have been treated in various works appearing since 1900, from personal narratives to analyses by Chinese scholars long after the fact. This book outlines as simply and briefly as is respectable the events of that historic uprising.

Christopher Martin
Castleton, Vermont
September 9, 1967

1 | SEEDS OF REBELLION

To understand the modern China of the last half of the twentieth century, one must study the events of the end of the nineteenth century, for what happened in China then set the stage for a state of mind that has governed Chinese thinking ever since.

In China, that state of mind is often referred to by the awkward word "anti-foreignism." The feeling began in the sixteenth century, and finally led, in 1900, to an open rebellion against attempts of Europeans and the Japanese to degrade the Chinese and their society. Anti-foreignism had not ended even when the Communists conquered China in 1949.

All through the years of the Republic of China, which was founded in 1912, anti-foreign feelings continued, although largely submerged. The hostility existed in the days of Sun Yat-sen and those of Chiang Kai-shek. Resentment against foreigners resulted in occasional riots by members of the government. And after the Chinese Communists won the war against the Nationalists, the anti-foreign attitude still persisted. It was an important part of the continuing Communist revolution in the nineteen-sixties, when the notorious Red Guards ran riot throughout the cities and countrysides of Communist China. One of the primary aims of the Red Guards was to stamp out foreign ways and foreign influences in China, whether American, English, Japanese or Russian. In a very direct way, the Red Guards of the sixties were the heirs of the Boxers of the last days of the nineteenth century and the early months of the twentieth century.

Traditionally, throughout history, the Chinese and their leaders have regarded themselves as a superior people. Until the last half of the twentieth century little was known in the Western world about ancient China, and, because the Chinese spoke in such superior terms of their civilization, it was generally believed that the civilization predated that of the Western world. Since the end of World War II this belief has been shown to be untrue. The civilization of China is not so old as that of the Fertile Crescent in Asia Minor or of the Indus valley in India. Chinese methods of dating and confusions about the reigns of various dynasties conveyed the wrong impression to early students from the West.

The impression persisted because China was long isolated by her high ranges of mountains, deserts and great plains. She alternately welcomed and turned out foreigners; welcoming them when they first came and turning them out when they attempted to seize power over her. She built the Great Wall to protect herself from the hordes of Mongols beginning in the third century before the birth of Christ. But the Mongols were not the only ones to threaten

China. As early as the seventeenth century, threats came from the West. Before then, the Chinese Emperors had alternately opened and closed China's ports to Western trade, depending on the behavior of the Westerners.

In 1684 the Emperor K'ang Hsi of the Manchu dynasty opened all the ports of China to Western trade. This is where our modern story begins, because the Manchu was the last of the dynasties, a rulership imposed from outside the Great Wall by the royalty of Manchuria, which was not regarded earlier as part of China proper.

To understand the impact of the West on China one must go back beyond the dynasty of the Manchus, called the Ch'ing dynasty, to the last Chinese dynasty, the Ming, and study in some detail the coming of foreigners from the West.

Ming can be translated as "brilliant" or "glorious," and that is an apt description of the three-hundred-year dynasty founded by the Emperor Chu Yüan-chang in 1368. The Ming dynasty became the master of all that we call China proper, and its tentacles extended into Mongolia and as far south as Ceylon. Its form of government was taken over by the succeeding Ch'ing, or Manchu, dynasty and lasted as long as the Empire. During the reign of the Ming Emperor Yung Lo (1403-1424) China carried on trade with Java, India, Japan and other nations of Asia. In the beginning of the sixteenth century the Europeans arrived in Asia – the Portuguese first – and began to establish trading posts. They settled on islands off the coast of Kwangtung province and in ports in Fukien and Chekiang provinces.

This first meeting of cultures was definitely a failure and had an effect on all that happened later: The Portugese who came to Asia were lawless men who spent much of their time pillaging the cities and towns of the Chinese coast. Finally the people and the government became sick of them and took action. A Portuguese settlement at Ningpo was wiped out by a massacre in 1545 and so was a trading colony in Fukien in 1549. The Portuguese were then driven out of China except that they retained possession of a handful of tiny islands south of Canton.

From this experience the people of China came to look upon the foreigners as "devils" and to distrust them completely.

The next Westerners to come to China were the Dutch, who arrived in 1622 and captured part of Formosa. They were driven out finally, and the Westerners were even more deeply suspect in the eyes of the Chinese.

In the sixteenth century the Jesuits came to China as teachers and students and they were better received. Matthew Ricci, a Jesuit priest, arrived in China in 1582 and lived there until he died in Peking in 1610. In those twenty-eight years he did more to win respect for Westerners than any other man or group of men. He adopted Chinese ways and learned the Chinese language. He dressed in Chinese robes and he studied the classics. He was honored by the Emperor with some degree of confidence, and Jesuits were assigned to the Imperial Bureau of Astronomy to reform the Chinese calendar.

The English first came to China in 1673 when a squadron of five warships arrived at Canton and destroyed the Chinese batteries that tried to keep them from coming into the city to trade. Always, it seemed, the foreigners came to China with sword and lance, and always they brought trouble.

So by the middle of the seventeenth century, when the decaying Ming dynasty fell before the onslaught of the

Manchus, the Chinese people had definite cause to dislike and distrust foreigners.

To understand the later reaction to foreigners, one must also know the Manchus – who they were and what they became.

The Manchus were a Tungusic people, related to the Chin people of Asia, who had been the most ferocious opponents of the Sung dynasty, which ruled China from 960 until 1279 A.D. The Manchus, then, were a people largely Chinese in culture and related to some of the northern Chinese in blood lines. In the beginning of the sixteenth century, the Manchus were living in the Sungari valley, in what are now the provinces of Kirin and Heilungchiang in Manchuria. In a quarter of a century the Emperor Nurhachu had extended his frontiers as far as the Amur river on the north, and captured Mukden from the Ming Emperor. Adopting Chinese ways, the Manchus created the dynasty they called "Ch'ing" which means "pure."

These fierce northern warriors often broke through the Great Wall of China and raided the North China plain, but they conquered China only when the Ming dynasty had become old and weak.

In the sixteen-forties, a young man named Li Tzu-cheng became a brigand, driven by famine and the high taxes imposed by the government of Shensi province. He became more than a bandit, for he was followed by thousands of men who also had been driven to desperation. In 1642, Li captured Kaifeng and proclaimed himself master of Shensi. Two years later he declared himself the first Emperor of a new dynasty, marched on Peking and captured the city. The Ming Emperor hanged himself as the troops of Li marched into Peking.

It seemed then that China was to have another Chinese

dynasty, but it was not to be. Li Tzu-cheng had murdered the father of a Chinese general named Wu San-kuei, and this general was in charge of the northern defense of China against the Manchus. In revenge for the murder, he joined forces with the Manchus, led them through the Great Wall and into battle against Li's troops near Peking. The Manchus defeated Li, and with Wu San-kuei's help, soon were in control of Peking.

The adherents of the Ming dynasty kept fighting for fifteen years, but by the end of 1650 the Manchus had secured control of most of China. They were wise enough to adopt Chinese ways, although they kept themselves apart from the Chinese as a people. In manners and customs they accepted only part of the Chinese practices, while forcing some Manchu practices on the Chinese. The wearing of the queue, for example, was a Manchu custom. The Chinese were forced to shave parts of their heads and wear this headdress as a symbol of their loyalty to the government.

The Manchu pride and the forced wearing of the queue created some opposition in China, but this must not be overestimated. The Manchus left the Ming administrative system very much alone, kept the Ming officials in power and began to win their loyalty. They were wise enough to cultivate the educated people, and Chinese and Manchus alike were appointed to new offices and competed in the Imperial civil service examinations. Soon the great majority of positions in the bureaucracy were held by Chinese, including some of the highest posts.

Actually, the very factors that made the Manchus acceptable to the Chinese people eventually brought about the fall of the Empire. In their eagerness to keep China loyal, the Manchus were ultraconservative in observing the old forms. They embraced Confucianism. They made sure that the roads to power in the Empire lay through the civil service examinations, and so the educated youths followed a tightly prescribed course of education to win the degree that would bring them wealth and honor. They frowned on originality, whether Manchu or Chinese. They frowned on experimentation with social customs. In short, the Manchus attempted to keep China just the way it was, even as the foreigners were knocking at the gates, bringing new ideas that had been proved in their ability to produce material wealth.

The story of the rise and fall of the Manchus is the story of the emergence of modern China, with all its ingrown attitudes of superiority and fear of the outside world.

When the British and the Dutch came to China in the seventeenth century to open trade, they established the important trading center of Canton by building factories there for the processing of Chinese goods, such as tea. By the middle of the eighteenth century, Canton was the central trading point of China with the West, and in 1757 the Emperor Ch'ien Lung recognized this by making Canton the sole point of trade. During these years, trade was carried out by the British East India Company, for the most part, and it was reasonably satisfactory to all concerned.

The British, realizing they were foreigners in China, showed no animosity toward the Chinese custom of kowtowing to representatives of the Emperor. (To kowtow was to show obeisance by bumping one's head on the floor.) Nor was there any objection of the traders to petitioning the Chinese rulers as though they were gods.

But in the middle of the nineteenth century, the East India Company was dissolved, and the British government sent official emissaries to China to arrange for new conditions of trade. These government officials refused to accept the old Chinese forms of paying honor to the Emperor and a dispute began that was, in a way, the start of troubles between the East and West, and the basis for Chinese anti-foreign sentiment.

The Manchus and their Chinese officials had no understanding of the civilization that had risen in the West so far away from them. They did not realize that the Industrial Revolution of the eighteenth century had created vast markets among the new middle-class Europeans for the goods of better living. The beneficiaries of the Industrial Revolution expanded their creature comforts. To meet the needs, the businessmen of Europe needed sure supplies of goods and raw materials. As long as trade could be arranged on favorable terms, the Manchus and the Chinese people were safe enough from the foreigners, but the Manchus did not realize that they faced nations stronger by far than themselves; they were used to wielding the power of life or death over every person in the Chinese Empire. The Manchus were arrogant and weak. The Europeans were arrogant and strong. The result was war.

Britain was accustomed to intercourse with other nations on the basis of equality, and the British soon objected to the Chinese conviction that all other people were tributary to the Emperor. British traders objected to high Chinese taxes on imports and exports. Soon each country began to regard the other warily.

The issue was complicated by the traffic in opium. Opium

had been used in China for many years, but the Chinese court banned its use early in the eighteen-hundreds. The laws were violated by British traders and Chinese officials until 1838, when Peking appointed a new Imperial commissioner named Lin Tze-hsu to stamp out the opium traffic. Lin arrived at his post in Canton in 1839 and began to act with great vigor, first ordering that all contraband drugs be surrendered and that foreign merchants promise to stamp out the traffic. To win acceptance of his demands he virtually imprisoned the whole foreign colony in its own quarters. More than 20,000 chests of opium were handed over and destroyed, but the British withdrew from Canton and moved to Macao and then to the island of Hong Kong (which was then nearly uninhabited).

Further friction developed and in November, 1839, an armed clash occurred between British and Chinese warships at Hong Kong. The British began to attack Chinese ports from Canton north to the Yangtze, and in July, 1842, they captured Chinkiang where the Grand Canal crosses the Yangtze and so cut an important line of communication for the Chinese. They were preparing to assault Nanking when the Chinese came to terms.

The resulting Treaty of Nanking, signed August 29, 1842, opened five ports to the British. They were Canton, Amoy, Foochow, Ningpo and Shanghai. The treaty also provided for the opium destroyed by the Chinese, and for other concessions, including land concessions.

From this war, with the concessions forced by the Europeans, came the belief in Manchu and northern Chinese circles that the Europeans were no better than barbarians.

Many Europeans came to China then, to trade and to

live. They did not understand the languages, they did not understand the customs. By their own wishes, and the wishes of the upper-class Chinese, they lived apart from the people. The poor Chinese became their servants. The rich Chinese ignored them and they ignored the Chinese. Such organizations as the Peking Club and the Tientsin Club were formed on Chinese territory, employing Chinese servants, serving Chinese foods cooked in Western style – but Chinese guests and members were not welcomed. In the beginning, this separatism was quite satisfactory to the Chinese, but as the Europeans gained power in their country, it became a source of annoyance and later of hatred.

Little by little, parts of China's outlying Empire were hacked away from the control of the Manchus. Soon the Portuguese took Macao. Russia took away the part of China's Empire north of the Amur river, and later took Turkestan. France seized Tonkin, to the south. Britain seized Burma, which had been a Chinese dependency.

All went well for a time, but in 1856 came another war, called the Arrow War. In October of that year a ship, the *Arrow,* was boarded by Chinese officers at Canton and most of its crew were arrested on the charge that they had been engaged in piracy. The ship was owned by a Chinese and had a Chinese crew, but its captain was British, it was registered in Hong Kong and it flew the British flag. The Chinese officials hauled down the British flag and took possession of the ship. The British declared that their flag had been insulted, but the Chinese refused to give any satisfaction.

Neither side would compromise and at the end of a month the British began hostilities against China. They captured the forts that commanded the approaches to

Canton and bombarded the viceroy's headquarters. The Chinese retaliated with a declaration of war. Later France joined the war and Canton was captured, and Great Britain, France, the United States and Russia made a number of demands on the Peking government. The government ignored the demands, and several fleets went north and captured the forts at Taku. The British and French then threatened to march on Peking itself, and the Chinese government yielded to the demands of the foreigners. It signed the Treaties of Tientsin, which opened ten more ports including some in Manchuria, gave foreign ships the right to use the Yangtze river, let foreigners travel wherever they wished in China and guaranteed the freedom of Christians to practice and propagate their religion.

The growing weakness of the Manchu dynasty caused the foreigners to take ever greater chunks of Chinese territory. In turn, this state of affairs created resentment among the Chinese against their Manchu masters. Also, the foreigners brought new ideas. This caused some Chinese to become pro-Western and others to become violently anti-Western, bringing rebellion for both reasons.

Christianity brought unforeseen problems to the Manchus. A Chinese scholar named Hung Hsiu-ch'uan began studying Protestant teachings, not as a Christian but as a Chinese student of a foreign philosophy. He developed a sect of his own called the Worshippers of Shang Ti, which was a combination of mixed-up Christianity and Chinese beliefs. In time this cult became political in nature. It attempted to overthrow the Manchu dynasty and set up a new dynasty called T'ai P'ing, or "great peace." The revolutionaries began marching in 1850 and in 1853 they captured Wuchang and Nanking.

This T'ai-P'ing rebellion was an attempt to reshape China

along Western lines. It was a rebellion against the old ways, a struggle of peasants against landlords. The rebels talked of land reform, reduction of taxes, better status for women and elimination of corruption in government. The rebellion was put down by the Manchus, who were assisted by the conservatives of Chinese society, but the rebels held Nanking for ten years and put some of their ideas into effect in this region.

From this rebellion came a deep suspicion that foreign ways would bring the destruction of the Empire and strong opposition by the conservatives to Christianity. But from this rebellion also came one positive development: the realization by some of the ruling group of the Manchus that China must follow the West in the development of its railroads, roads, telegraph, and modern ships and armies. However, as this began in the 1880s, it was already too late, because the Western world and the Japanese were casting envious eyes on the territory so long controlled by the Chinese Empire.

In the eighteen-nineties came the Sino-Japanese War, in which China lost control of Korea and Manchuria. The French became actual rulers of parts of Southern China, as did the British. Germany seized a colony in Kiaochow in central Shantung province.

China was soon split in many directions. Theoretically, the Manchu Emperor controlled the country. Actually, he controlled the region around Peking and Tientsin, and, through warlords who professed loyalty to him, he controlled the remainder of the country in name only. What the foreigners wanted, they took. What they wanted, for the most part, was goods for trade bought at phenomenally cheap prices by European standards because the living

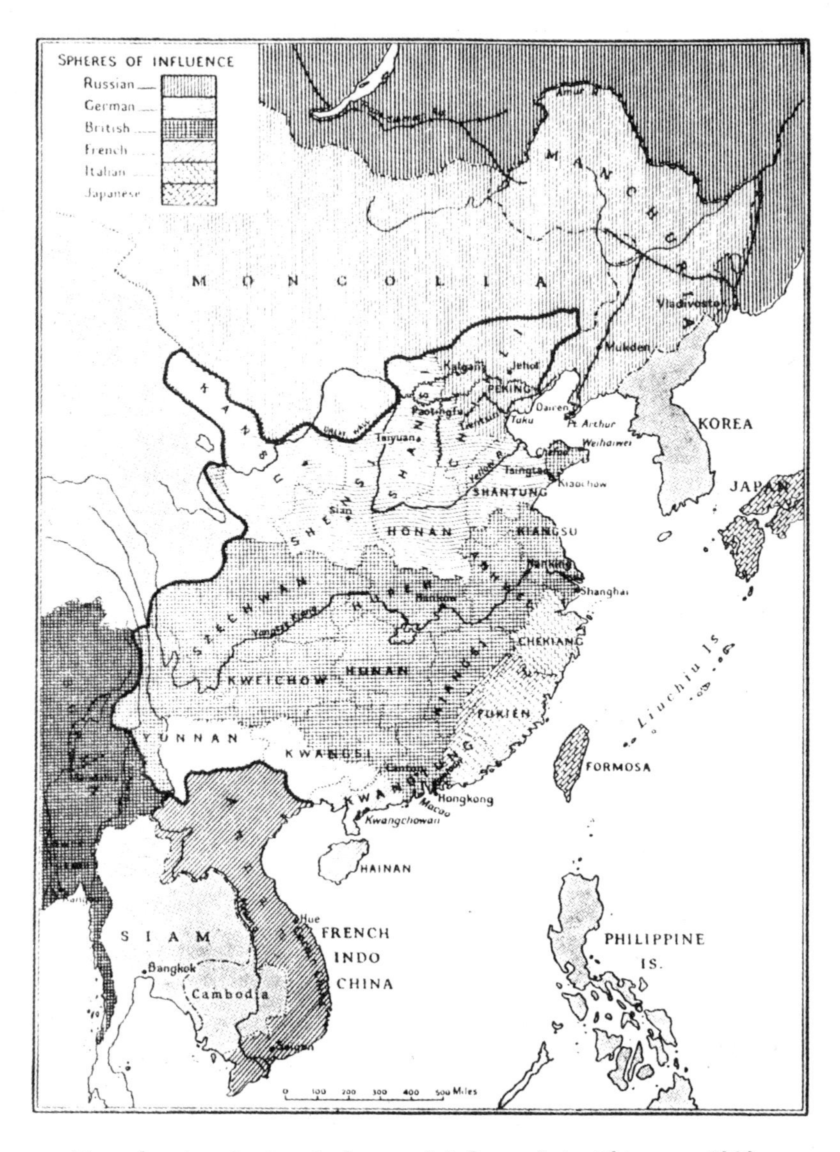

Map showing foreign "spheres of influence" in China, c. 1900.

standard of China was basically no better than the minimum needed to sustain life among the peasants.

Before 1900, Westerners and Chinese were talking about the day China would be cut up like a melon by the foreigners. There was no doubt that the foreign governments intended to seize actual colonies. What kept them from doing so was their intense rivalry with one another, rather than any strength of the Chinese government. Yet in Peking, the great northern capital of the Celestial Empire, the Manchus fooled themselves into believing that they were strong and that Chinese ways could overcome the foreign ways. The Westerners, on their part, did not realize that the revolutionary ideas they were pressing on China must run into conflict with ancient Chinese ways of doing things.

After 1860, when the missionaries flocked to China, Christianity became the greatest source of annoyance to the Chinese government and the conservatives among the Chinese people. The missionary's teachings ignored the customary respect paid to family ancestry, and in this it seemed to threaten the basis of Chinese society, which was the family. But the missionary was only a foreign teacher; the real wrath of the Chinese who followed the old ways was turned against those Chinese who took up the new.

The conservatives charged that these Chinese Christians were setting out to undermine the entire structure of Chinese life. Actually, in many ways the impact of Christianity and other aspects of Western life forced the conservative Chinese into new adherence to the Manchus, when otherwise they might have worked against the Manchus.

Toward the end of the nineteenth century Chinese society was split in two, with the conservatives turning more every day against all manifestations from the Western world, and the modernists seeking and accepting what they found useful in Western ways.

In a sense the Boxer Rebellion can be said to be the unconscious reaction of all who either hated the West or who were seriously disturbed by the breakdown of the old society. This wave of revulsion explains why in the latter stages of the rebellion many Chinese who were not rebellious or anti-Christian by nature took part on the side of the Boxers. It also explains why moderate-minded officials took the part of the old Dowager Empress and the scheming generals in this reaction against the West.

China had its progressive leaders. Li Hung-chang, among the Emperor's most trusted officials, was one of them. After the T'ai-P'ing rebellion, he encouraged the building of arsenals, dockyards and warships. But no few men could do the job, faced with the long Chinese tradition. In 1895, Li Hung-chang went to Japan to negotiate the treaty that ended the Sino-Japanese War. He admired what he saw in Japan, for Japan had begun modernizing her ways less than a half century earlier. He summed up the problems of his China in a talk with Japan's Prince Ito.

"My country is hampered by traditions and customs," Li said. "One can hardly do what one wants . . . China also has people who understand modern affairs; but there are too many provinces with strong sectionalism. . . ."

Li Hung-chang was too loyal to the Manchu Empire to mention another serious difficulty in China: the power struggle within the Imperial family. This struggle dated back to 1862, when Emperor Hsien-feng died. He had taken as a concubine a very intelligent girl named Tz'u Hsi, who became important in Chinese affairs when she bore the Emperor a son, because the Empress, Tz'u An, had no son.

The son, T'ung Chih, was named heir to the throne. Tz'u Hsi managed to become a regent of the Empire, and schemed her way into almost total power by killing off the three princes who had also been appointed regents. Tz'u Hsi even dominated her own son, T'ung Chih. When he died at a very early age she was able to place on the throne her three-year-old nephew, Kuang-hsu, the son of her sister.

The old Dowager Empress retained control of China during the days that Kuang-hsu was growing up. She was interested in power for herself, and she never lost a chance to kill off an enemy or to cement that power. Her life was a constant round of scheming, and because of her schemes the Empire stagnated.

When Kuang-hsu came of age he began to fret under the controls of the old woman, and the struggle for power in the Imperial Palaces began. It was a deadly struggle, but a very polite one. The Dowager Empress always talked in courtly terms of love and protection, and the Emperor talked of his filial piety toward the old lady. Yet, beneath it, they were bitter enemies.

Late in the eighteen-nineties, a reformer named K'ang Yu-wei began petitioning the Emperor for reforms in the government. In 1895, after the disastrous defeat by the Japanese, these petitions at last came to the ears of the Emperor, and the young ruler paid sympathetic attention to them. That summer the Emperor called the attention of the Dowager Empress to the petitions and some talk of reform was begun. It came to little.

Two years later K'ang came back to Peking with more

petitions for reform. He came when the Germans were moving in on the Kiaochow peninsula, and after some discussions the reforms were begun that summer. They included Westernization of the army, establishment of an Imperial University, modernization of schools and change in the old manner of appointing officials to government on the basis of their scholarship in the traditional language and literature, rather than on their ability to do the job at hand. Commerce was to be promoted. Students were to be sent abroad at government expense to study languages and foreign ways. The government agencies were to be consolidated and much waste wiped out.

The Emperor wanted to make these changes, but the Dowager Empress said that the ancestors of the Manchus had not made them and so they should not be made. The Dowager Empress moved to cut down the Emperor's power by ruling that officers appointed to government by the Emperor should appear before her to "express their gratitude." This, of course, gave her final say in appointments, because if she did not like an appointment she simply refused to see the applicant, and he could not serve without having paid his respects.

Finally, when one of the Dowager Empress's followers defied a decree of the Emperor, he abruptly dismissed the man, along with a number of other appointees of his aunt's. Then came an open struggle between the Dowager Empress and the Emperor. His supporters appealed to a progressive general, Yuan Shih-kai, realizing that the Empress was preparing to seize power from the Emperor. But Yuan Shih-kai had only 7,000 soldiers, while General Jung Lu, loyal to the Empress, had 100,000 soldiers. Yuan's army was modern and so were his ideas, but he was not foolish

The Empress Dowager

enough to brave these odds. The young Emperor, believing in reforms, was sacrificed, and the Empress had him confined in a palace on an island in the Forbidden City of Peking. She took over rule of the country, after the reform movement had been at work for only one hundred days.

The Dowager Empress then began to fight against foreign domination in her own way. In 1899, she supplanted the Emperor (as we shall see), as punishment for his crimes against her. Prince Tuan, a member of her court, persuaded her to have his son, P'u Chin, named heir to the throne. The army was strengthened and drawn in around the north and central provinces of China, and the military men began following an anti-foreign policy. With the Emperor imprisoned and helpless, China began behaving as if she were indeed a strong power, capable of resisting the demands of the Westerners.

In this period the Chinese people grew very restless, particularly in Manchuria and in Shantung province. In Manchuria, the Russians were likely to use force whenever a Chinese village resisted their demands. In Shantung province, if the Chinese villagers refused to do what the Germans told them to do, they could expect to find their villages burned to the ground by German troops. Then, too, there was conflict between the Chinese Christians and the Chinese believers in the old ways of ancestor worship, and the missionaries often interfered in disputes among Chinese in favor of their Christian believers. This action resulted in the Christians getting what they wanted at the expense of the old believers. It also brought about a growing hatred of Christianity and foreigners by simple villagers.

The Chinese, who saw foreigners coming to live in splendor in their country and who resented it, had for many years formed themselves into protective societies and some of these societies were very much opposed to foreigners. Among these was a group called the I Ho Ch'uan, or the Society of Righteous and Harmonious Fists, which became a volunteer militia organization. It was later to be called the Boxer movement, because the members of the secret society performed athletic exercises much like those of boxers.

The Boxers, and other societies like them, received much encouragement in 1898 and 1899 from the Dowager Empress and the court at Peking. It was realized at Peking that the army forces must be strengthened, and some officials believed that these secret societies could provide the nucleus of a trained militia force, which in turn could be used to back up the standing army in disputes against the foreigners.

And so, throughout the parts of China loyal to the Peking government the militia groups were encouraged and grew in 1899. Chief among them was the I Ho Ch'uan, or Boxer society.

This organization was far more than a simple club. Its members participated in secret rites and were bound to each other in the same manner as the Italian secret societies. Those who joined such a secret society must obey all its rules; violation of the rules was punished by death of the member and perhaps even the killing of every member of his family.

Secret societies had existed in China for many centuries, to serve many purposes. They had been wiped out from time to time by the authorities at Peking, but they always came back. In the secret society the Chinese found a way of banding together against oppression, whether from foreigners, agents of the central government or the throne itself. The societies survived because they served a definite purpose to the people below the upper ranks of Chinese society.

Shantung province became the central stronghold of the Boxers in this period, largely because the foreigners were most active there in 1898 and 1899. The Germans had taken the Kiaochow peninsula. To the north, the British had occupied Wei-hai-wei. The Yellow river, which flows through Shantung, had overflowed and caused much misery in the province, and there was good opportunity for the secret societies to make themselves popular with the people there by struggling against the foreigners and blaming all the ills of China on them.

In 1898, in Shantung and along the border of Chihli province (where Peking is located), there were a number of incidents in which Chinese Christians and missionaries were injured or killed by the anti-foreign, anti-Christian Boxers. Houses and chapels were burned in Weihsien and in other towns. Government troops answered the attacks, and the Boxers were caught and identified.

In the spring of 1899 a new governor came from Peking to take charge of Shantung province for the Imperial family. He was Yu Hsien, an able official but very anti-foreign in his sentiments. It was said by the Boxers that he looked favorably upon their society and upon their anti-foreign activities. In some cases they were allowed to terrorize whole districts, such as the district of P'ing yuan where, in October, 1899, about 300 Boxers looted the homes of Christians and fought a battle with government troops from Tsinan.

When Governor Yu Hsien learned of this battle, he discharged the district magistrate who had sent in the troops. He also dismissed the local commander of troops and imprisoned the constable who had arrested a number of the Boxers. The Boxers cheered the governor and began pillaging Christians throughout the province. Yu Hsien did nothing when Boxers terrorized Tsinan, Chining and several other large cities and towns.

Finally, the foreigners in China protested in Peking, and to save face – because the Dowager Empress could not admit she encouraged anti-foreignism – Governor Yu was replaced. His replacement was General Yuan Shih-kai, and the governorship was the general's reward for having betrayed the Emperor to the Dowager Empress. Instead of refusing to save the Emperor and fight the Dowager's army, Yuan Shih-kai had disclosed the plot to deprive the Dowager Empress of her power and had assured his own advancement in the army under the old lady's rule.

Yuan Shih-kai came to Shantung and issued a strong proclamation against the Boxers. Had he carried out the plans he announced in the proclamation the Boxers would have been wiped out and suppressed quickly enough. But, as was often the case with the Chinese, the strong proclamation was for show, not for action. Yuan issued private orders that no force was to be used against the Boxers, or anyone else who rose up against the foreigners and Chinese Christians. These orders came directly to Yuan from the Imperial Throne in Peking. The Dowager Empress was taking a hand, and she was encouraging the Boxers.

The Boxers were dispersed in Shantung, but they were not suppressed. In Chihli province, which included Peking, it was quite a different story. In 1899 and 1900 the Boxers became very powerful there. The Dowager Empress encouraged this growth of their power as long as they used it to embarrass and harry the foreigners.

The foreigners in Peking should have been warned of events to come by several happenings in 1898. On October 23, 1898, an American doctor named Robert Coltman, Jr., was called to the railroad town of Fengtai on the Hangkow-Peking rail line. Dr. Coltman was professor of surgery at the Imperial University and he held many other honorable posts. He was professor of anatomy at the Imperial Tung Wen Kuan (foreign language university), surgeon for the Imperial Maritime Customs and surgeon for the Imperial Chinese Railways. It was in this last capacity that he was called to Fengtai. A coolie working on the rail line had been run over by the express train from Tientsin and his leg had to be amputated.

Dr. Coltman went to Fengtai that day and performed the operation. Later he stopped for tea at the house of the resident engineer on the line, an Englishman named A. G. Cox. That afternoon the resident was going to make a tour to inspect the new Lukouchiao bridge, built across the Hun Ho near the famous Marco Polo bridge, to carry the rail line. Dr. Coltman had an engagement that day in Peking and had to return.

On the following day Dr. Coltman received a telegram from Fengtai, asking him to return at once because Cox had been wounded, along with another European, in what the telegram described as a "riot" at Lukouchiao. The telegram had been sent a few hours after the doctor's departure, but had not arrived in Peking before nightfall. Because the city gates were closed for the night, no attempt had been made to deliver it.

Dr. Coltman hastened to Fengtai. There he treated Engineer Cox and Captain Norregaard, the builder of the bridge, and heard their story.

Cox had taken a trolley down the rail line to Captain

Norregaard's house, which was near the bridge. The two had then joined some other foreigners and had gone to look at the bridge. Near the eastern entrance to the bridge stood a group of soldiers from Kansu province. They had recently come into Chihli and were very strong in their talk about the foreigners they saw before them. They kept using the words *yang kuai tzu,* which meant "foreign devil."

With the group was an Englishman who was an official interpreter for the British Embassy. The interpreter, who spoke Chinese fluently, talked to the soldiers and asked them to step aside so the foreigners could do their job. The soldiers refused and told the foreigners to go away.

A Chinese officer came up and the interpreter told him to quiet the men. The officer said they were not his troops. The interpreter said he would hold him responsible anyhow. The officer told the troops to let the foreigners through their lines. They did so. The officer then disappeared.

There were four men in the English party. They inspected the bridge and then returned, to be met by a hail of stones from the soldiers on the eastern side. One man threw a stone that hit Cox. The engineer chased him, caught him and knocked him down. The mob then turned on Cox and bowled him off his feet. Captain Norregaard was hit with a stone too, as he went to Cox's assistance. He then drew the revolver he was carrying and fired two shots into the crowd. The soldiers ran away.

Two days after going to Fengtai to dress the wounds of the Europeans, Dr. Coltman was called to meet with the governor of Peking, Hu Chih-fen. The governor said he had been ordered by the Dowager Empress to investigate the riot at Lukouchiao. He asked the doctor to go with him, because the Chinese troops had reported that the foreigners shot two soldiers and wounded them severely. The action had been taken without provocation, the army officers had reported to the Imperial Palace.

Dr. Coltman accompanied Governor Hu and about 20 retainers to the station at Lukouchiao, and there the investigation began. First the watchmen at the bridge were questioned. They told the same story that Cox had told Dr. Coltman. Then the party walked to the inn at the village of Lukou. There the doctor and the governor drank tea while they waited for the generals and colonels of the army group to arrive to testify before the Dowager Empress's commissioner.

When the army officers arrived they showed very little respect for the governor or the foreign doctor – quite unlike the usual usage of polite Chinese to others. The general, a Kansu soldier named Chang, told the governor he need not have come at all. One of the colonels then began a tirade against foreigners and railroads. Dr. Coltman understood every word because he had spent fifteen years in China and spoke fluent Mandarin, but it was so unusual for a foreigner to speak fluent Chinese that the army officers talked quite openly against foreigners in front of him. These were the troops of the famous Moslem General Tung Fu-hsiang, who had been ordered by the Dowager Empress from far-off Kansu to support her anti-foreign policy.

The object of the trip had been to see two wounded men who were supposedly lying at death's door, because they had been shot by the foreigners in the affair at Lukouchiao. The men were brought out by very reluctant soldiers, only after Governor Hu's firm and repeated demand. Dr. Coltman saw that one of them was uninjured and that the other had a superficial wound in the shoulder.

On his return to the capital Governor Hu sent a Memorial to the Empress. (A Memorial was a written document addressed in very flowery language to the throne. Since only a handful of the highest officials were ever allowed to enter the Forbidden City and set eyes on the royal family, the usual means of communication between the ruling figure and the people was the Memorial. Even Memorials were never seen by the ruler unless the most trusted advisers decided that the person offering the Memorial was of rank high enough to be heard.)

In his Memorial, or report, the governor said that the army men had been rude to him when he represented the Dowager Empress, thus showing disrespect for the throne. The Dowager Empress issued an edict depriving the rudest officer of one step of his rank, and she commended Governor Hu for his action.

When General Tung Fu-hsiang heard that his officer had been degraded, he became furious and threatened to leave the capital and take his troops back to Kansu unless Governor Hu was removed from office and the offending officer restored to rank. The Empress, who needed the Kansu soldiers more than an honest governor, did as Tung Fu-hsiang demanded. General Tung's troops now began swaggering about the streets of Peking in their red and black uniforms, taking what they wanted from carts and stalls and insulting foreigners when they saw them. Tung Fu-hsiang formed an alliance with Prince Tuan, the arrangement for the succession of P'u Chin was announced on January 24, 1900, and to the more knowledgeable of foreigners it was apparent that there could be nothing but trouble ahead between the representatives of the West and the Imperial Court within the Forbidden City.

2 | THE BOXERS

Even in the second half of the twentieth century there is some argument as to the manner in which the Boxer organizations of China began, but there is no argument as to their nature by 1900. Whatever they were to begin with, by that time they had become dedicated to the destruction of the Christian religion in China, the murder of foreign and Chinese Christians and the removal of foreign influences.

For many months, as the Boxers gained strength, the foreign diplomats in Peking were lulled by their own beliefs as to the state of affairs in China. In part this was because anti-foreignism and anti-Christian feeling were not entirely new. In 1895 an organization known as the Chitsaiti, or Vegetarians, had massacred several Protestant missionaries in the town of Kucheng, in Fukien province to the southeast. They were tried for their crimes. In the trial it became apparent that a number of Chinese were trying, indirectly, to involve the Manchus in a movement to eject all foreigners from China.

The Boxers organized themselves into local clubs, with the avowed purpose of improving physical fitness by exercising. Secretly their leaders prepared rites and incantations. One of the principles of the Boxers was the belief that if they were armed with their faith, followed the prescribed rules and fought against the Christians, they could not be killed in battle. They believed that bullets would turn away from their holy bodies as they marched forward. From the standpoint of the leaders this belief was extremely valuable, because it gave them soldiers who were absolutely unafraid.

The Boxers were not alone in their hatred of foreigners during the early eighteen-nineties, and that is why it was so easy for them to grow quickly, recruiting members of other secret societies which had the same policy: Drive the Westerners out of China.

In Chihli province, the center of the Empire, the Jesuits reported that in the town of Hien Hien, in the spring of 1898, they had seen a placard posted on a prominent corner for all to see. It said:

NOTICE

> The patriots of all the provinces, seeing that the men of the West transgress all limits in their behaviour, have decided to assemble on the 15th day of the fourth moon and to kill the Westerners and burn their houses. Those whose hearts are not in accord with us are scoundrels and women of bad character. Those who read this placard and fail to spread the news deserve the same characterization. Enough! No more words are needed.

This anti-foreignism was not basically anti-religious in nature — the Chinese were always a most tolerant people in matters of religion. But the missionaries, unfortunately, could not resist their opportunities as foreigners to meddle in the affairs of the Chinese people, and on the village and town level of Chinese society the basic contact with foreigners was with missionaries. That is why the anti-foreignism in China took a religious overtone.

The Boxers progressed.

One day, in the spring of 1900, another placard appeared, this one in a prominent place in Peking. It said in part:

> So, as soon as the practice of the I Ho Chuan [Boxerism] has been brought to perfection – wait for three times three or nine times nine, nine times nine or three times three – then shall the devils meet their doom. The will of heaven is that the telegraph wires be first cut, then the railways torn up, and then shall the foreign devils be decapitated. In this day shall the hour of their calamities come. The time for rain to fall is yet afar off, and all on account of the devils.

In the spring of 1900 the Boxers had organized in nearly every province, and they were extremely strong in Chihli, because a weak governor had allowed them to grow. Chihli became the central point of the unrest.

The first major clash between the Chihli troops and the Boxers came in the Laishui district in May, 1900. A thousand Boxers were assembled at the village of Kaolo. The fact that so many Boxers were allowed to gather in one relatively small place indicated the strength of the Boxers and the weakness of the provincial authorities. The Boxers had learned in Shantung province that they had nothing to fear from the Dowager Empress. Every time Yuan Shih-kai indicated that he was going to pursue the

Boxers, the Empress issued a new Imperial edict ordering him to go slow in his campaign and to "reason with them."

So when the Boxers assembled in Kaolo they were unrestrained. Soon riots broke out. Seventy-five houses belonging to Christian Chinese were burned and sixty-eight Christians were killed. There had been trouble before – a few months earlier the Christian missionary S. M. Brooks had been killed by Boxers in Shantung – but there had been nothing as serious as this riot.

A few days later provincial troops encountered the Boxers in a pitched battle. Eighteen Boxers were killed, but later the government troops were ambushed and their commander was killed. This was the first time that the Boxers had killed an official of the Chinese government, and the foreigners and the people waited to see what the throne and the provincial authorities would do.

The governor of the province was timid. In a Memorial to the governor, the Imperial Throne again cautioned for moderation and against "rash actions." The Boxers then knew that they had the approval of the Dowager Empress to continue to harry the foreigners and their Christian disciples.

This riot at Kaolo might be termed the jumping-off point at which the Boxer Rebellion became inevitable.

The Boxers in Chihli province now turned their attention to the telegraph lines and the railroads, as had been indicated in the Peking poster, because these modern facilities represented the foreigners to the Chinese people. On May 27, 1900, the Paotingfu railroad line was attacked and the telegraph line alongside it was torn down. In a hundred-mile stretch from the Liuli river to Ch'anghsintien, all stations, bridges and factories along the line were attacked, burned and destroyed. Railroad communication between

Peking and Tientsin was cut off. At this point even Governor Yu Lu of Chihli became upset. He telegraphed the Tsungli Yamen (Foreign Ministry), reporting that the Boxers had become too aggressive and urging that the Imperial Throne order them suppressed.

The Tsungli Yamen represented what the Boxers hated. It was the organization that dealt with all things foreign, within and outside the country. It had been formed in 1861, replacing the old Imperial Bureau of Barbarian Affairs. The Tsungli Yamen in 1900 was an important part of the Chinese government, and its chiefs were supposedly very sympathetic to modern ways.

Until this point the Imperial Throne had been considering organizing the Boxers into a militia force to protect China against the foreigners. The Dowager Empress had refused to take seriously the reports that the Boxers would attack foreigners anywhere, even right under her nose in Peking.

In spite of the warnings of foreigners like Dr. Coltman, who spoke fluent Chinese, moved about among the Chinese and understood what was happening in China, the foreign diplomats in Peking had refused to become upset about the future. And so events moved on.

On the evening of May 28, 1900, the day after the attack on the railroad line, the Western diplomats in Peking held a meeting to decide what they should do for their own protection.

They were now thoroughly frightened. They had learned that General Yang Fu-t'ung had been killed and that his Chihli troops had then joined the Boxers. The diplomats demanded action. The Tsungli Yamen promised that a strong Imperial edict would be issued at once, and the diplomats' fears were partly allayed.

Map of the province of Chihli, showing the area in which the major fighting took place (between Tientsin and Peking).

As the diplomats met, elsewhere in Chihli province groups of Boxers also met, bowing low to the ground, kowtowing three times toward the east and three times toward the south and then throwing themselves upon their backs. After this they arose and began their boxer exercises, which included warding off imaginary blows.

The next day, May 29, it was learned in Peking that the rail line had again been cut, this time at Fengtai, the place close to the city (just two stations below Peking on the Peking-Tientsin line) where Dr. Coltman had journeyed in the incident that now seemed so long ago. All the foreigners along the rail line had fled to Tientsin for safety. The foreign diplomats decided to call in marines and other guards from the foreign warships that happened to be standing off the Taku Bar.

The Tsungli Yamen was informed, but the Yamen asked that the foreigners delay their call for guards because the Chinese armies would protect them. By this time the foreigners had become very suspicious. Dr. Coltman and others knew that Boxers were coming into the city in large numbers and that they were being housed in the palaces of a number of the princes in Peking. This information could mean only that the Boxers had at least semi-official support from within the Forbidden City. It was frightening news, because it was known that the Boxers intended to kill all foreigners in China.

On June 1 the first detachments of foreign troops began to arrive from the seacoast. They were 75 Russians, 75 Britons, 75 Frenchmen, 50 Americans (marines), 40 Italians and 25 Japanese.

The foreigners were now getting ready for serious trouble. What they did not realize was that the trouble was upon them, and that it had already gone too far to stop.

3 | THE CONFLICT BEGINS

On the last day of May, 1900, a party of French and Belgian railroad engineers en route from Paotingfu to Tientsin encountered a party of Boxers about twenty miles outside Tientsin, a big trading city of north China. In the battle that followed, four Europeans were killed. When the survivors dragged their wounded into Tientsin, a party of Russian Cossacks was dispatched to hunt down the Boxers and rescue the missing members of the European party.

The Cossacks found the Boxers, engaged them in battle and killed many of them in this first open encounter between Boxers and armed European soldiers. When this news became known, the Boxers of Chihli province went into a frenzy and began agitating for the deaths of all foreigners.

On June 4 the Huangtsun station on the Peking-Tientsin line was destroyed by the Boxers. At this point, troops of the Imperial government intervened and tried to put the Boxers down. Chang Chih-tung, viceroy of the Empress at

Hankow, telegraphed Peking that in the guise of anti-foreignism the Boxers were staging a revolution against the throne. Soon some responsible parties in Peking began to believe that this was true, although in the capital city the Imperial Court refused to consider the Boxers as enemies of the government.

In Peking, with the arrival of the foreign marines and soldiers, few as they were, the diplomats and foreign residents felt more secure. There were still differences of opinion. The French minister, Stephen Jean-Marie Pichon, had been the earliest to sense the coming of trouble; the British minister, Sir Claude MacDonald, had sensed it last and was not even yet quite sure that matters were serious. The United States minister, Edwin H. Conger, seconded the British minister in his ignorance.

While they were arguing, the Dowager Empress was telling her ministers that the only reason the Boxers were firing on Chinese troops was that they looked like foreigners. She continued to appease the Boxers because she, too, disliked the foreigners. She sent an emissary to be sure that the government troops did not fight the Boxers in Chihli, and consequently, by June 14, the Boxers were actually in control of the province. On June 10 Prince Tuan was appointed President of the Tsungli Yamen, the foreign office. Since Prince Tuan was sympathetic to the Boxers it was apparent to any who knew the situation that the lives of all foreigners in China were very much in danger.

By the end of the first week in June the foreigners in northern China were very much alarmed. On June 8 all the missionaries in and around Peking abandoned their own compounds and sought refuge in the Methodist Mission a half-mile east of the United States legation. They brought many converted Chinese Christians with them, for the lives of the Chinese Christians were as much forfeit as those of the foreigners. The defenders began fortifying the Methodist Mission with barbed wire.

Fortunately for the foreigners, under the rules laid down by the Imperial Throne years earlier, the foreign diplomatic missions were all confined to one area of Peking, so the 450 guards and marines of the various nations were able to keep a guard on Legation Street and in the quarter to protect the people from the Boxers.

With the change in personnel at the Tsungli Yamen there was no further question in the minds of the foreign diplomats about what they must expect from the Imperial government. On June 10 the Tsungli Yamen asked the foreigners to refrain from calling for assistance from the ships in the harbor at the Taku Bar. The foreigners refused. Sir Claude MacDonald had already sent an urgent telegram to Admiral Sir Edward Seymour calling for dispatch of troops to Peking. The next morning, June 11, an international force of 1,950 men left Tientsin by train. They met the Boxers halfway beween Tientsin and Peking, at the town of Langfang. The crisis was now to become a war.

Admiral Seymour had landed immediately on receiving the messages from Peking and arrived on June 10 in Tientsin from Taku with 500 British sailors and marines. Russian and French troops joined the force there, and three trains set out for relief of the worried foreigners in Peking. The first train was filled with sleeping cars for the troops and construction material to repair the line in case the Boxers had done serious damage to it. Before the force left it had risen to 1,950 men, including Germans, Russians,

Admiral Sir Edward Seymour, leader of the allied expedition to Peking.

British, French, Japanese, Austrians, Italians and Americans. The force was well-armed, with eight machine guns, six small field guns and one six-pound gun mounted on a flatcar.

On June 11 all was quiet. The force moved slowly up the rail line, making sure that the rails had not been cut or the ties removed.

On the afternoon of the second day, however, the relieving trains were attacked by a large force of Boxers, who came rushing at the foreigners, secure in their belief that their incantations and faith would prevent foreign bullets and foreign swords from hurting them. The Boxers were armed only with swords and spears and a few old rifles. The troops opened fire and killed about 50 Boxers. The rest retreated.

The allied force proceeded, with one train going back to Tientsin for supplies, and patrolling the line to keep it open. The main force found it could only go as far as Langfang, because at that point the Boxers had torn up the rails.

Here the Seymour expedition encountered the Imperial troops and here the war began.

As soon as the Seymour expedition had left Tientsin the people of northern China began to learn of this move of foreign troops toward their capital. On the night of June 10 the British summer legation outside Peking was burned to the ground. On the night of June 11 Chancellor Sugiyama of the Japanese legation was killed at the main gate of Tientsin. On June 13 a large force of Boxers entered Peking and began to burn churches and foreign compounds. The American Board Mission was burned. The two Catholic churches known as the South Cathedral and the East Cathedral were burned. The American Presbyterian Mission, the Society for Propagation of the Gospel compound, the International Institute and the London Mission compound were all burned in the next few hours by whooping, shouting Boxers who murdered any Chinese who tried to stop them or any Chinese they thought were Christians.

If there were moderates who wondered why nothing was done by the Imperial Throne to prevent the burnings on June 13, it was only because they were not party to the counsels of the Dowager Empress.

For two days the officials of the Tsungli Yamen had tried to prevent the foreigners from bringing troops to Peking. They promised that the Imperial armies would protect the foreigners and their property. But the foreigners in Peking no longer believed the Tsungli Yamen and they would not halt the reinforcements.

On June 13 the Imperial Throne issued a new decree, ordering the army of Nieh Shih-ch'eng to the railroad area to guard against foreign advance. The Dowager Empress spoke through her commander, Viceroy Yu Lu. "If again there are foreign troops attempting to go north by train," she said, "it is Yu Lu's responsibility to stop them. Let Nieh Shih-ch'eng prepare his troops for any emergency."

Here at Langfang the emergency appeared. The Imperial troops faced the foreign relief expedition, and neither would give way. That same day Admiral Seymour's communications with Tientsin were destroyed. The city was surrounded by Imperial troops and Boxers.

At this point the Imperial troops and the Boxers were still functioning as separate entities. In Peking the Boxers were roaming the streets, attacking foreign installations

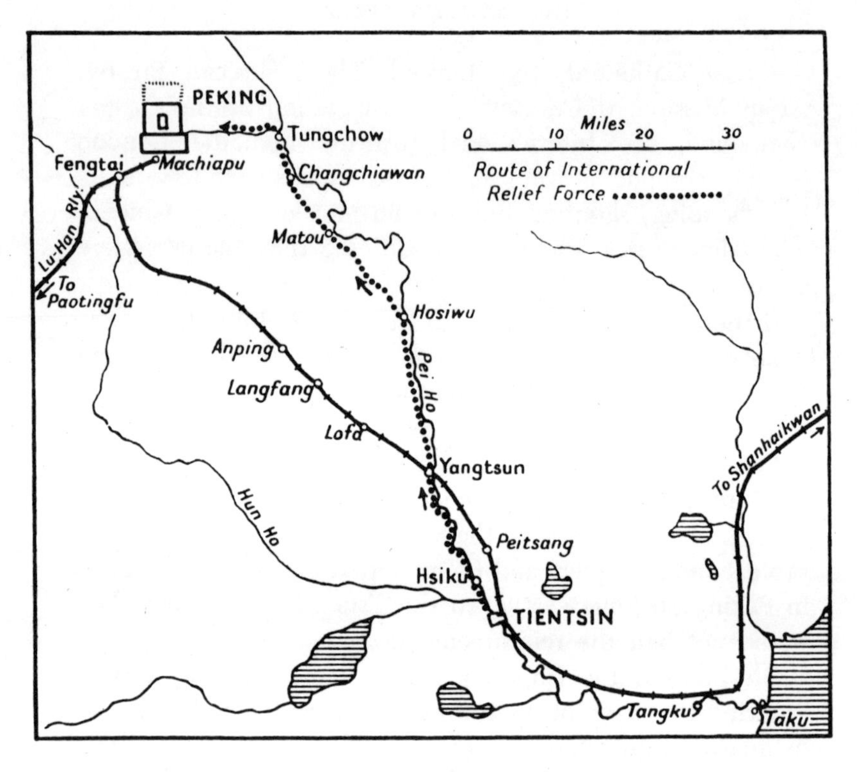

Map showing the route of Admiral Seymour's expedition.

and surrounding the foreign legation compound on Legation Street, where hundreds of foreigners and Chinese Christians had taken refuge. The foreigners, by and large, took the position that their siege began on June 7, when the first outbreaks of violence against them were reported. Night after night, the marines and soldiers repelled with fire attempts by small groups of Boxers to break into the foreign compounds.

On June 14, as Admiral Seymour was stalled and out of communication with the naval authorities at Taku, the foreign naval commanders in the area held a meeting to decide what they must do. They decided it was important to seize the Taku forts and the railroad station at Tangku so they could keep communications open with Tientsin. The next day was set for the seizure.

Dr. George Nye Steiger, one of the earliest serious students of Chinese affairs in the West, called what happened in the next two days a "drift toward a war" that neither side really wanted. On the Chinese side was Viceroy and Governor Yu Lu, who was charged with the responsibility of handling the affair, since it occurred in Chihli, his viceregal mandate. Yu Lu, on June 14, was concerned with the protection of the missionaries and, secondarily, with defense against foreign troops. The next day the order of importance was reversed. On the foreigners' side, the senior naval officers of the various Western naval detachments became concerned with the safety of Admiral Seymour when his communications were cut off. By June 15 they had decided to act drastically.

Actual hostilities between the Chinese and the foreigners broke out, then, on the night of June 15, when the foreigners moved to attack the Chinese forts at Taku. Much has been made of the fact that the Chinese fired the first shot; yet the first aggressive action was taken by the foreigners, and there is no question about it.

In the councils of war that preceded the landings against the forts, the United States commander, Admiral Kempff, refused to participate in the landings on the ground that the Chinese had committed no act of war against the foreigners. In other words, the Americans took the position that to land and take the forts would be an act of war, and they refused to participate in striking such a blow.

The foreign naval committee, for that is what it was, drew up an ultimatum to the Chinese defenders, demanding the surrender of the Taku forts by 2 o'clock in the morning on June 17. Copies of the ultimatum were prepared for the fort commanders and for Viceroy Yu Lu, who was at Tientsin.

As soon as the ultimatum was prepared the Western naval men readied themselves for war against the Chinese in the forts. The Westerners sent armed landing parties ashore from the ships. The gunboats were moved up into the shallow waters of the Pei Ho, within easy range of the forts. The railroad station at Tangku was occupied by foreign troops — a hostile act. The ultimatum was dispatched on June 16.

The Chinese did nothing until about an hour before the ultimatum was to expire. Then the forts opened fire on the ships anchored in the Pei Ho. Several of these shots were fired in the direction of the U.S.S. *Monocacy*. The American gunboat had aboard a number of refugee missionaries and did not take part in the battle of the forts but, from that moment on, Admiral Kempff took the position that the Chinese had committed a warlike act against the United States, and so justified American participation in later events.

About thirty foreign warships lay outside the Taku Bar in the deep water, but could not come into the shallow Pei Ho. Inside the bar, in the river, about ten miles from the big warships were the small vessels facing the forts. They were gunboats and destroyers: the British H.M.S. *Algerine*, H.M.S. *Fame* and H.M.S. *Whiting;* the German gunboat *Iltis;* the French *Leon;* the Russian *Bobr*, *Koreech* and *Gilyak*. All but the *Fame* and *Whiting* were gunboats.

The first shots were fired at 1 A.M., and then the gunboats began to reply.

Meanwhile, in Peking events also moved steadily toward war. At noon on June 16 the bridges into the Forbidden City were abustle with sedan chairs and scurrying retainers of the princes and lesser nobles who frequented the palace. The Imperial Council had been summoned into session at noon to deal with the serious situation in which the Dowager Empress found herself. This council was attended by all the Manchu princes, all the dukes, the high nobles, Chinese officials and members of the various boards and ministries of the Imperial government.

The Empress Dowager, sitting on her Peacock Throne, asked her ministers and advisers what policy she now ought to adopt toward the foreigners. Riots had broken out in the city, she said. A foreign force of soldiers was heading toward Peking.

One minister spoke openly. The Boxers should be driven from the city by force, he said, then the trouble would be over and the foreign troops could be told that there was no reason for them to pursue their course.

Prince Tuan, the friend of the Boxers and enemy of the foreigners, spoke up quickly, shouting the minister down.

Yuan Ch'ang, one of the officials of the Tsungli Yamen, said that the Boxers were an evil force. They were revolutionaries, not patriots, he said, and their invulnerability to Western bullets and sword cuts was a fiction.

The Dowager Empress interrupted Yuan.

"If we cannot rely upon the supernatural formulas, can we not rely upon the heart of the people?" she asked. "China is weak; the only thing we can depend upon is the heart of the people. If we lose it, how can we maintain our country?"

The Dowager Empress revealed here the basic dilemma of the Manchus. They, too, were foreigners, and they were much despised by elements of the ancient Chinese nobility. The Dowager Empress's willingness to delude herself about the nature of the Boxers is much more easily understood if one knows that she felt very uneasy about the Manchu dynasty's future. Overlooking the brutalities and anti-government actions of the Boxers was quite politic for her. At least it had seemed politically sensible until the Boxers went too far and infuriated the representatives of the Western powers.

Now the Empress had her way again. She ordered the Boxers recruited into the army, thus putting the Imperial stamp of approval on them and their actions. War was truly inevitable. That same day, as the ultimatum sped from the foreigners at Taku to Viceroy Yu Lu, so did an Imperial edict ordering him to resist any military action by the foreigners. It was apparent in Tientsin that those first shots would be fired, and by late afternoon of June 16 Yu Lu had given up any hopes for peace.

Once that fatal first shot was fired from one of the Chinese forts, the war was begun. Forts and gunboats traded shots until dawn. The destroyers *Fame* and *Whiting* moved up the river and captured four Chinese torpedo boats. The landing parties made ready to storm the forts, and when a magazine in the south fort was blown up, and fire from both forts slowed down, the landing parties broke the Chinese defenses and stormed into both forts.

On that afternoon of June 17 events moved very quickly in three places. In Tientsin the Imperial troops began bombarding the foreign settlements, assisted by Boxers. In Peking the Imperial Council met again to decide on action. Halfway between, the Seymour Expeditionary Force was attacked for the first time by Imperial Chinese troops.

In Tientsin the Boxers had been trying to burn down the foreign settlements since the night of June 15, and most of the women and children of the foreign community had been evacuated by special armed train to Tangku station, which was held by the Western troops. But not all foreign women and children could leave, and 120 women and

A captured Taku fort.

138 children were ordered to take shelter in Gordon Hall, the municipal building of the British settlement. The Boxers had mounted scattered attacks on the night of June 16, and had destroyed most of the French settlement. On June 17, at 3 o'clock in the afternoon, the bombardment of the foreign settlements began in earnest, coming from the main fortifications in the city.

On the afternoon of June 17 the Imperial Chinese troops surrounded Tientsin and the siege began. There could be no further communication either with Taku or with the Seymour force because rail and telegraphic communications had been destroyed.

The foreigners in Tientsin were well-protected. A force of 1,700 Russian troops had come down from Port Arthur to join the Seymour expedition in the relief of Peking, but the Russians had arrived late and so were on hand inside the Tientsin wall when the fighting broke out.

The Chinese opened fire from the fort in the city *yamen* (city hall), and from the Military College across the river. A mixed force of Austrians, British, Germans and Italians volunteered to attack the Military College and did so, taking the position that afternoon and stopping the gunfire. Meanwhile, the Russian troops dispersed about the foreign compounds to stave off other attacks, and with their four fieldpieces began replying to the Chinese gunfire from the Yamen.

Communications between Peking and Tientsin were cut off for both foreigners and Chinese. Thus, when the Imperial Council went into session on the afternoon of June 17 the Dowager Empress and her advisers did not know that hostilities had already begun in the southern city. When she convened her advisers in meeting that day, the Dowager Empress was furious. She had just received a four-point ultimatum from the foreigners in Peking, she said. It called for a special place to be given the Emperor for residence (outside the Dowager's power), future collection of all Chinese government revenues by the foreigners and future military control of all China by the foreigners. The fourth point she did not mention – restoration of the Emperor to rule.

Actually, there had been no such ultimatum. Apparently it was a fabrication prepared by Prince Tuan to push the Dowager Empress into war. Tuan hated the foreigners more than anyone else in China did, because he had persuaded the Empress to make his son Heir Apparent to the throne and the foreigners, by refusing to recognize his son, had stopped the murder or exile of the Emperor. Tuan was desperate for war.

At this meeting of the Imperial Council, Prince Tuan had his way. The Dowager Empress ordered three officials to go to the foreign diplomats and tell them that if they wanted war they should haul down their flags and leave Peking. A decree was sent to the provinces, ordering troops to be sent to Peking.

"If we must perish," said the Dowager Empress, "why not fight to the death?" She was now prepared for war. She did not know that it had already broken out.

The same communications failure beset Admiral Seymour and his force, so the first they knew of the commencement of hostilities came at Langfang when Imperial Chinese troops opened fire on them on June 17. The Chinese were armed with Mausers and quick-firing field guns, and they took refuge behind the walls of the town and villages nearby, using smokeless powder that made it difficult for the Europeans to find their enemy.

The Chinese force opposing the Seymour expedition was

obviously a very strong one. Faced by it, the admiral decided to retire to Tientsin, for he had few guns, little ammunition and very little food because he had expected to move quickly to Peking, normally less than half a day's journey by rail.

So war came to China and the foreign colony without a declaration of war or any real intent on either side to wage war. Chinese and foreigners alike acted as they did from fear of the others, whom they understood so badly.

4 | THE BATTLE OF TIENTSIN

By June 19 there seemed to be no unanimity of action anywhere that would indicate exactly what was happening. Some members of the Tsungli Yamen still talked of peace. The Dowager Empress, although persuaded to a course that meant war, still talked of peace. The diplomats in Peking talked of peace. In Tientsin, Chinese and foreign soldiers fought and killed one another. Along the Tientsin-Peking rail line, the Seymour expedition began fighting its way back toward Tientsin, not knowing that the Chinese Imperial forces had surrounded the city. Everywhere there was confusion and lack of information.

At five o'clock in the afternoon on June 19, the Tsungli Yamen distributed identical notes to every foreign legation in Peking. The notes called on the foreign diplomats to prepare to depart from Peking within twenty-four hours, because of the capture of the Taku forts and the warlike acts of the foreigners in Taku harbor. The diplomats and their families were told that they would have a military escort to take them to the coast.

The foreign diplomats immediately called a meeting to decide on a course of action. They sent a note to the Tsungli Yamen stating that it would be impossible to move so fast. They also asked for an interview.

The next morning no answer had been received so the diplomats met again and talked over their problem. All but one decided that war was inevitable, and that they must await rescue by their soldiers. They decided against trying to communicate further with the Chinese government, but began making plans for a siege by fortifying the legation area as much as possible.

The one dissenter was the German minister, Baron von Ketteler. He decided that he would go to the Tsungli Yamen and try to reason with the officials there. He set out for the Yamen, accompanied by his secretary and two guards, and had almost reached the building when he was shot and killed by a Chinese soldier.

The German minister's death settled matters for the foreigners. They received more messages from the Tsungli Yamen but they paid no further heed to them. Before the day was over, Chinese troops had begun firing at the legations and the Boxers were no longer restrained.

If some foreigners wondered what had happened to the Seymour expedition, they need not have held hope for rescue from that source. All day long, on June 18, the Seymour force had fought superior-sized enemy units, and the fighting continued after dark. On the morning of June 19 the Seymour group decided to abandon the railroad as too dangerous, because they discovered that they must fight for every foot of progress and were severely restricted in their defense as long as they stayed on the railroad. They also learned that the bridge over the Pei

Ho had been destroyed, and that they could not take their trains into Tientsin. So the Seymour force abandoned the trains and took to junks on the river, trying to make its way back to Tientsin.

In Tientsin there were new difficulties for the foreign military men. The Chinese brought two field guns up to the railway embankment on the other side of the Pei Ho, facing the British concession. (Such concessions were pieces of ground wrung from the Chinese in the succession of treaties signed over the years. They were occupied by business and shipping firms, and were subject to the law of the nation occupying the land, not to the laws of China. They were, in effect, tiny colonies within China owned and operated by the foreigners.)

Commander Beatty, of the British ship *Barfleur*, with three companies of sailors, went across the river to attack the guns, but the Chinese defenders were well dug in and the attack failed. Beatty and three other British officers were wounded.

A nine-pound gun was brought up by the British and it shelled the Chinese position continually until the Chinese guns were withdrawn that night.

Even then the British concession was in constant danger and was under fire all day and all night, because there were plenty of houses on the other side of the river to protect the Chinese. The British concession was barricaded and sandbags were piled along the streets to protect the foreigners.

In the Yamen fort the Chinese had forty-five field guns of various sizes, and these fired on the foreign settlements constantly. There was also a battery of seven guns at the Lutai canal, two miles from the railroad station, and there were two guns a few yards from that point. The Military College had been destroyed, but the Chinese brought another pair of field guns into some ruins behind the college, and trained these on the foreigners. There were many other guns — so many that the foreign concessions were subjected to fire from seven different directions.

The major problem of the garrison in the foreign settlement was a lack of guns. There was plenty of food and plenty of water to withstand a siege, but the troops did not have heavy weapons to counteract those of the enemy.

One piece of good fortune came early. The Germans had a small steam pinnace in the river, but it had been struck by a Chinese shell and disabled. The pinnace had drifted over against the bank at the Military College and had stuck there. The Chinese could see it and they could see its Maxim machine gun, which was undamaged. Yet the Imperial troops did nothing to capture or disable this weapon. The British decided to go and get the gun.

The steam pinnace of the *Barfleur* was given the job. With a crew of six volunteers the pinnace went across the river, under constant fire from the Chinese, and tried to tow the German boat back. When three of the crew had been wounded, the British gave up the idea and were forced to retreat without the gun. That night two volunteers swam across the river in the darkness and brought the gun back in a Chinese sampan, a small shallow boat. This gun was then mounted near the Astor hotel in the foreign settlement and trained on the two Chinese guns that fired from the ruins behind the war college.

The foreign garrison was besieged for more than a week, with crowds of angry Boxers milling about the streets at the edge of the sandbag revetments, and shouting and shooting at those inside. The Chinese had about sixty guns altogether. The defenders had only seven 12-pound Russian field guns and a 15-pound Maxim Nordenfeldt gun, which had very little ammunition. The danger of being overrun by an attack was serious at all times.

The danger ended on June 24 when a force of 2,000 British, American and Russian sailors, marines and soldiers made its way from Taku to the Chinese lines. The column forced its way into the city, bringing two Russian batteries of 15-pound guns and a gun from one of the French ships in the harbor. A few hours later a British group arrived bearing another 12-pounder.

All during this siege the Seymour expedition was making its way slowly back from its fruitless attempt to relieve Peking. The junks to which they had moved their supplies and arms had to be dragged along the riverbank with ropes, and the men on the towpath were fired upon by the Chinese constantly as they pulled their way along. After a few hours of this the expedition was reduced to holing up and fighting off attack in the daytime and travelling and fighting at night. On June 20 they were running seriously short of food and began killing stray ponies and donkeys they found on the water path. They had no fresh water and were forced to drink the river water, contaminated with filth in which floated the dead bodies of Chinese Christians who had been massacred by the Boxers upstream.

On June 21 the string of junks came to the point of crisis. All day long the junks were subjected to heavy fire and the food was gone. That night the troops made a forced march, knowing that they must come to some end before the next day was half over, because they were growing short of ammunition. At daybreak they reached the Hsi-ku arsenal, and after a brief struggle the desperate foreigners captured the arsenal and a large supply of food and ammunition. But here the Seymour group was stranded, surrounded by Chinese troops who now made desperate attempts to recapture the position.

On June 21 the Chinese made two attacks on the arsenal, but were repulsed. They attacked again at sunrise on June 22 and this attack was also repelled. The foreigners then trained the heavy guns of the arsenal on the adjoining fort, which was held by the Chinese, and on the surrounding villages. They kept up a heavy fire, which in turn prevented further attacks.

That night two companies of British marines were sent out to try to make contact with the Tientsin garrison and bring a relief force. They were almost immediately met by the Chinese and forced back with heavy casualties. That same night, however, the Chinese servant of one of the foreigners agreed to carry a message to Tientsin.

He made his way safely through the Chinese lines and to the city. There the Russians and others had just arrived, and the next day a force under command of Lieutenant Colonel Shirinsky of the Russian army, fought its way to Hsi-ku and rescued the Seymour group, blowing up the arsenal before they left.

That allied force had been away from Tientsin for 16 days. Of the total force, 295 men had been killed or wounded – more than ten percent of the total – and the only effect of its action had been to convince the Chinese Imperial government that the foreigners were bent on capturing the Imperial capital.

The foreigners began bringing in more arms and men

from Taku. On June 27 British Brigadier Dorward arrived with a force that included a Hong Kong artillery regiment. That same day the Russians attacked the Peiyang arsenal on the side of the river opposite the foreign settlements. The arsenal was well-defended and the attackers were forced to move across an open plain to reach it. They were driven back by the Chinese in their first attempt and called Tientsin for reinforcements. At ten o'clock that morning a British naval brigade came to help, and this time the Americans got into the fight, bringing in a marine artillery unit. An hour after the reinforcements arrived, a lucky shell hit a magazine that contained eighty tons of powder. The magazine blew up with such force that the explosion was heard in Taku, thirty miles away. Not long afterward, a smaller magazine was struck and exploded, and the Chinese began a retreat, well-covered by fire from behind them. The foreigners occupied the arsenal then, suffering many casualties. The last defenders of the fort played a clever trick on the foreigners: They set off strings of firecrackers that sounded very much like rifle fire, and under cover of the fireworks escaped while the allied troops shot uselessly in the direction of the sounds coming from the arsenal.

Since the arsenal commanded the river, Admiral Seymour was able, after its capture, to evacuate the remaining women and children by water to Taku, where they could be cared for in safety aboard the various foreign ships. The troops under Admiral Seymour settled down to fight and wait for reinforcements.

5 | THE BATTLE OF TIENTSIN — II

During the next few days the most dangerous place in Tientsin was the railroad station, which the foreigners had occupied at the beginning of the troubles. They felt that the station must be held at all costs. The Chinese desperately wanted to capture the position and mounted assaults on it nearly every day after the battle of Tientsin began.

The railroad station was held by a force of Japanese, French and British soldiers. The Japanese and French occupied the station itself and the platforms. The engine house had been allocated to the British, who brought a Maxim machine gun into the position.

When the Chinese learned that a machine gun was opposing them, they brought up two nine-pound field guns to knock out the gun. They placed their guns in a clump of trees, about 1,200 yards from the engine house. Then the duel began. The Chinese could not advance frontally across the open 1,200 yards because the Maxim mowed them down. The men in the engine house could not rest or relax because they were under constant fire from the two Chinese guns.

The Chinese shooting was very accurate. One day they put eight shells into the engine house wall in a circle eight feet in diameter. This accuracy proved nearly disastrous to the British, for those shells broke through the wall finally and the last one killed and wounded seventeen of the Welsh guards who were on duty. Thereupon the defenders, except those actually working the Maxim gun, were ordered to lie down in the ashpit beneath the engine house floor, and there they stayed hour after hour as shells smashed into their building.

The French and Japanese had no such protection at the station and platform, but they brought in sandbags and built up barricades around the platform with loopholes for firing. They had to be constantly on the alert, because to one side of the railroad station there was a Chinese graveyard, which extended for three-quarters of a mile, and the mounds of tombs created excellent protection for the Imperial Chinese troops.

This protection was used one night at the end of June by a party of Boxers who crept up on the defenders at the station and managed to steal behind a group of boxcars that stood on a siding. They moved into a position between the station and the engine house, cutting off the two groups of defenders from each other. Most in danger were the Japanese and French at the station, because they could be surrounded and annihilated. Fortunately, even in the darkness of the night, a relieving force discovered the state of affairs that had developed and launched a night attack. The Boxers and regular Chinese troops rushed out for hand-to-hand fighting, and for a time the results were in doubt. Finally, the Boxers and the Chinese troops were driven back, but not before they had caused 150 casualties, mostly among the Japanese.

There were many incidents of heroic action on the part of the defenders of Tientsin, while they awaited the coming of the reinforcements who would save them. One such incident involved two British marines who had been wounded and left behind during the fighting for the Pei-yang arsenal. The men were told to await the coming of an ambulance that would pick them up and carry them to safety.

The two wounded men were cut off, however, by a force of soldiers and Boxers carrying a yellow banner and shouting slogans as they came. The soldiers came out between the railroad station and the arsenal and cut the wounded men off from retreat. One marine had suffered a terrible wound in the shoulder and could not walk. The other, not so badly wounded, picked him up to carry him, but then was wounded again in the calf and had to drop his companion. He escaped to the foreigners' lines, but the other marine was captured. Later his body was found, badly mutilated and with the head cut off.

Brutality was the rule on both sides. It was the Chinese custom to cut off the heads of dead enemies to show them to the authorities.

It was said that Viceroy Yu Lu paid a hundred taels to the soldiers who produced the heads of two American marines who fell in the advance of troops from Taku to Tientsin. On other occasions Chinese prisoners were captured while carrying bags that contained the heads of foreign soldiers. And the foreigners responded by killing every Chinese enemy without mercy.

After the first week in July some reinforcements began to arrive in Tientsin and the situation of the defenders improved. On July 9, Japanese General Fukushima arrived with a mixed force and cleared the Chinese from the houses around the racecourse. He then captured Haikwansu arsenal, which had been a very effective gun position for the Imperial troops.

Japan, Britain, the United States, Russia – all the nations that had interests in China – were very much aroused when they learned of events in Tientsin and Peking in June and July, and it was not long before troops began to arrive. Japan found it relatively simple to send soldiers and guns across the short water route. The Russians maintained a strong force in Port Arthur and they detached men and equipment for the task. The British began sending troops from India. The United States detached troops from the forces in the Philippines. Soldiers, sailors and marines of all nations were funnelled into Taku harbor at the end of June and the beginning of July. By July 13 several thousand troops were available for commitment to the battle, and they were well-armed. They had thirty-eight field guns, ranging from four-inch quick-firing fieldpieces to small mountain guns; and nine machine guns, all with plenty of ammunition.

On July 13 the allied commanders launched an attack on the Chinese in the native city of Tientsin, beginning at dawn with an artillery barrage. About 2,500 rounds of ammunition were shot into the city in a few hours, and it was not long before the Chinese guns were replying very slowly, which indicated the effect of the fire.

Under cover of the bombardment of the city, Japanese General Fukushima led an allied force of 5,000 men to a small arsenal on the western side of the Pei Ho river. Other troops were sent to the railroad station to reinforce the defenders there. Russian and German troops were sent along the east bank of the river to attack gun batteries on the Lutai canal.

When they saw the advancing forces, as dawn came up in the east, the Chinese opened a strong fire with rifles and muskets and inflicted a number of casualties on the main force. The object was to move to the cover of the arsenal walls, and from there to attack the Tientsin walled city. To do so, the troops would have to cross a wooden bridge over the canal and then traverse 2,300 yards of open ground to the city's south gate. A paved causeway ran straight from the city gate to the arsenal, which meant that equipment could be brought up over good terrain, but the land was open and the firing was fierce.

The French were the first to reach the bridge. They found that the bridge had been destroyed so successfully that they could not cross. Nor could they manage the sluices. They were pinned down under fire until the Japanese engineers could be brought up to repair the bridge. Then French and Japanese advanced together along the causeway until they came to a ditch six feet wide that ran at right angles to the causeway. Some troops were left in reserve. Forty men were sent to hold a cluster of huts above the ditch, there to give covering fire. Two hundred French and Japanese soldiers were sent along the causeway, until they reached a handful of houses on the outskirts of the city, about two hundred yards outside the city wall. Here they stopped. The Japanese engineers came up and built a long trench for protection. The attackers waited for reinforcements all morning.

On the left, British and American troops were brought up

to an advance point about 300 yards from the city wall, nearly to the corner where the south wall joined the west wall. They were quickly pinned down by the fire of Chinese cavalrymen entrenched 5,000 yards away, out of range of the small guns of the attackers.

Some of the American troops of the 9th Infantry division got into serious trouble at this time. Through some error in orders, they moved out ahead of the line of attack and were pinned down in a little Chinese graveyard just off the wall of the city, subject to fire from the entire length of the city wall and to a cross fire from the Chinese troops who occupied one of the small settlements between the wall and the French and Japanese forces. Two hundred Americans were involved in this desperate situation. They could not be rescued. They could not be reinforced. Two British officers were killed while trying to take ammunition to them by mule. The American soldiers could do nothing but crouch in the shelter of the Chinese grave mounds and pray as the Chinese fire made dust of the earth all around them. Before dark a handful of British sailors managed to worm their way up to the position to bring some needed ammunition and add to the firing against the city wall. That night they retired and counted the dead and wounded. Nearly a hundred of the Americans were casualties, nineteen of them killed.

One reason for the plight of the Americans was due to another mistake in orders. The bombardment of the city had begun at dawn, and when, after a few hours, the Chinese guns ceased to reply, the attack was slacked off. After the French and Japanese reached their position two hundred yards from the city wall, General Fukushima was told that they had actually breached the wall and held a position there. So that the allies would not be firing on their own troops, General Fukushima ordered the barrage stopped, and this change allowed the Chinese on the city wall to pour down strong fire on the attackers.

As night fell on July 13 the Japanese and French moved up and were reinforced. The Americans fell back from their untenable position in front of the line.

It had been hoped that the troops could carry the assault in a single day, but the terrain made this impossible. The approach to the city was along that causeway, and the causeway was only thirty feet wide. If troops moved across in close order, they were subject to devastating fire from the city wall. If they dispersed, it took a great deal of time to move a few men.

By nightfall the allied troops were in a disconcerting position. Some of them were standing in ditches, whose banks protected them from fire. But the opening of the sluices of the city's canal meant that the ditches were filled with dirty water, perhaps a foot or two deep. Some soldiers stood in this filthy water all afternoon, baked by the hot China sun, without water or food, waiting to move ahead.

At night, although the force had nearly achieved its objective, the situation seemed gloomy to the commanders. Losses had been high. The Chinese guns had not been silenced – it became quite apparent – because they began firing again and kept the causeway under shellfire so that it could not be used to mount a massive relief.

Just before dawn the Japanese engineers were sent out to make an attempt on the city gate. Lieutenant K. Inawe took a detachment with a charge of powder that was to be fixed against the gate. The plan was to run a wire back to the Japanese position and from there to explode the charge, whereupon the infantry would rush into the breach. But as Lieutenant Inawe moved forward he and his men were subject to a tremendous volley of shots from the city wall. One bullet destroyed the wire they had hoped to use to set off the charge. Lieutenant Inawe took the charge forward and blew it, quite expecting that he had undertaken a suicide mission. Oddly enough, although he was only a few feet from the charge when it went off, he was unhurt.

The soldiers rushed to the gate, only to find that it led them into an enclosure beneath the wall, and that they could not get through the inner gate on the other side. One soldier, however, had the presence of mind to climb the city wall and drop down the other side, and there he found that the Chinese defenders had fled at the blast, and he could open the gate from the inside. The city wall was breached.

Once the wall was breached the troops moved rapidly. The Japanese and one British unit were sent into the city itself, through the gate, to drive the Chinese defenders out the other side. Russians, Americans and other forces were sent around both sides of the city wall, to engage the Chinese wherever they might move out of the city. The British Fusiliers moved up to the north gate and advanced beyond that gate to the Grand Canal, where they captured several hundred military junks and a steamer. They took a small fort on the canal, which contained six guns that had never been fired.

In the city, the Japanese moved from street to street, mopping up remnants of the Chinese force. Most of the Boxers fled the city, leaving their red sashes and badges behind them, in case they encountered allied troops on the other side.

By the end of the day Tientsin was secure. The allies had lost about 800 men, most of them Japanese who had borne the brunt of the assault. The Chinese had suffered about 5,000 casualties, most of these caused by the heavy shelling of the city during the barrage.

Capture of the city itself did not secure the route to Peking or make the Taku-Tientsin road safe for the allies. While the city was under attack by General Fukushima, the Russians and Germans who had gone over to the other bank of the river circled around to the Lutai canal. They captured several batteries and achieved control of that waterway.

The allies expected the Chinese to fall back along the railroad and oppose their relief of Peking, but the Chinese Imperial troops did not do so at once. Nor did they defend the Yamen fort, the largest and most important in all Tientsin, from which they could have impeded the allied progress for some time. The Japanese captured the fort without opposition on the afternoon of July 14, complete with forty-five field guns.

The fall of Tientsin brought with it a most ignoble sequel, one the Chinese would remember for many years. Military control of Tientsin was divided into four sections, with British, French, Americans and Japanese in control of various parts of the city. A third of the city was in flames and there was serious confusion, but instead of moving quickly to establish order, the allies turned the city over for looting.

A few days after the fall of the city Viceroy Yu Lu died. He had been ordered to remain at his post although he had not agreed with the Boxers or the war, but he was so badly disgraced by the defeat that according to the Imperial Chinese custom he had no recourse but to commit suicide. All his family killed themselves at the same time, because the Dowager Empress was remorseless, and they knew that if they lived they would be degraded, and if they were not executed in Peking they would be thrown out of Manchu society.

Tientsin taken, the allies settled down to restore order to the city and to await the arrival of more foreign troops. It would be fall, the senior commanders believed, before they would have a force sufficiently strong to advance on Peking and engage the Manchus in the heart of their Empire.

6 | THE SIEGE OF PEKING

The siege of the foreigners in the legation district of Peking by the Boxers and Imperial army began on the afternoon of June 20, when the Imperial troops began firing on the foreign compounds. Yet, as far as the foreigners were concerned, their siege began much earlier, for they found it necessary to bar the doors to their compounds and guard the gates and the walls against attacks by the Boxers shortly after the first week of June.

On June 10 the foreigners in Peking received their last word from Tientsin – the hopeful message that nearly a thousand soldiers were on their way to the capital to protect the legations and the missionaries. By June 16 the troops had not arrived and the diplomats, unaware of the situation, began to fear that they never would arrive. That night the Boxers attacked the legation quarter, and the guards who had come up from Tientsin earlier were kept busy firing at them. That same night the Boxers burned the great city gate called the Chienmen.

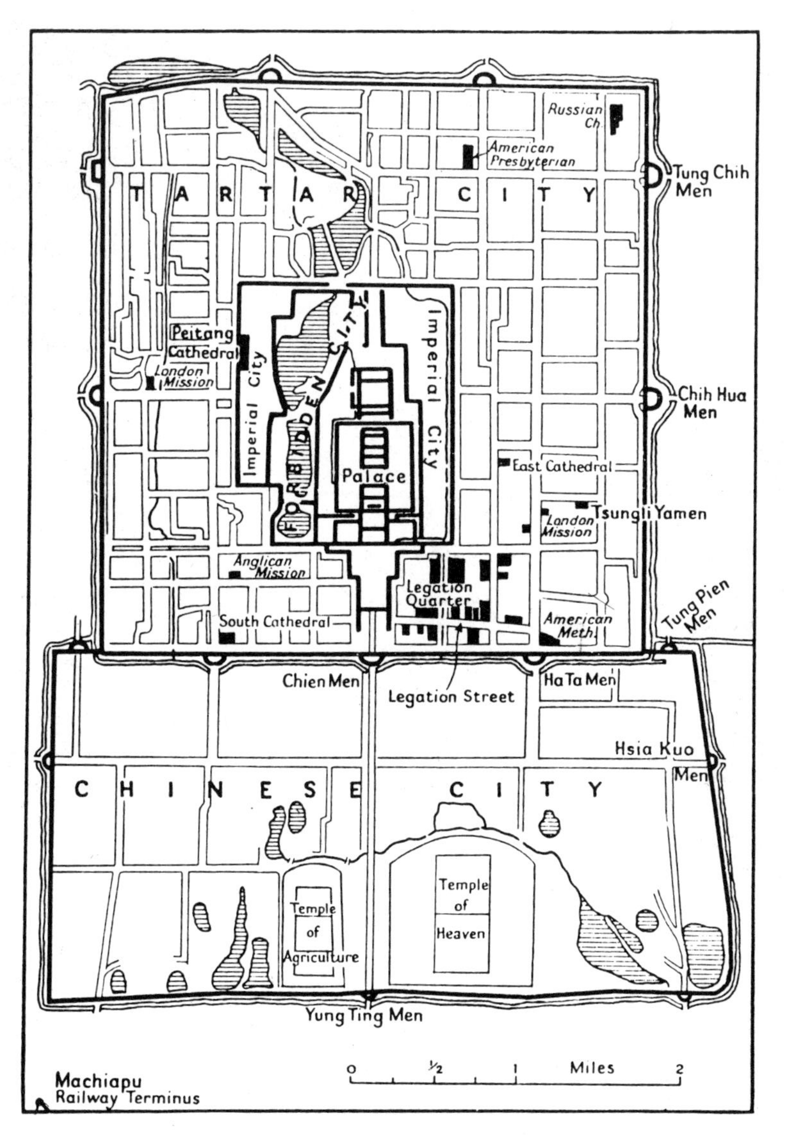

Diagram of Peking, showing the Legation Quarter and other foreign buildings, as well as details of the Forbidden City.

The Chienmen — the massive main gate to Peking.

The district into which all the foreigners were crowded ran up and down a single street, Legation Street, for about a half-mile. At one end of this east-west route stood the Russian legation. At the other end stood the Italian legation. Barricades were thrown up in the street at both ends and anywhere else that the Chinese might come through.

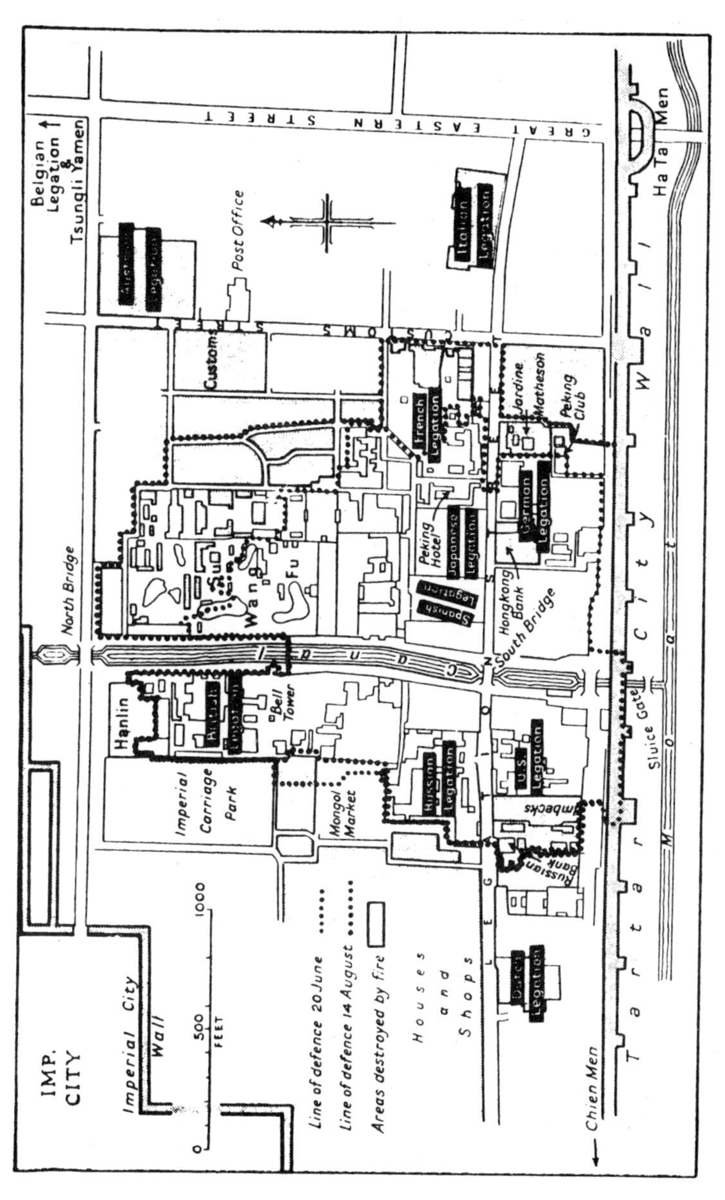

Diagram of the Legation Quarter, showing the lines of defense on June 20 and August 14, 1900.

The British legation, the largest in Peking, was off Legation Street, somewhat north of the others, closer to Chang An Street and the north bridge. At no point were the foreigners much more than a half-mile from the Forbidden City, which housed the Imperial Palace.

On June 17 the besieged foreigners learned the bad news: The Seymour column had been cut off and was forced to retreat toward Tientsin. Three days later, after the murder of German Minister von Ketteler, it was decided to send all the women and children of the foreign colony into the British legation. Carts were loaded with provisions from the three foreign stores in the legation district, and preparations were made for a siege. At four o'clock in the afternoon on June 20 the Chinese opened fire on the legations from all sides. But by this time, given a few days of warning, the foreigners had brought in enough provisions to last them for several months if necessary. Then the civilian men entered the British legation and began feverishly building sandbag revetments that should have been constructed days before.

The area to be defended ran north from the Tartar wall, which represented one edge of Peking, to the north bridge, encompassing the Peking Club and the German legation and part of the French legation. The Dutch legation was abandoned as too far from the center of activity.

The defense was organized around the British legation. A thousand coolies and servants, directed by the foreigners, began building sanitary and hospital facilities.

When the barrage began the principal attack was launched against the French and German legations. Chinese field guns were brought to a position only two hundred yards away, in the midst of a group of Chinese houses that fronted on Legation Street, around the Italian legation. The first day and night went well enough, although when they counted noses the foreigners discovered that instead of a thousand Chinese refugees in their midst they had two thousand, including a number of students and Christians who would be massacred if they were turned out to face the Boxers and the troops.

All day on June 20, and again on June 21, Chinese and foreigners were set to work making sandbags for fortifying the British legation and the weak places in the compound

A sandbag barricade in the British Legation in Peking.

walls along Legation Street. About 20,000 sandbags were made in all.

On June 21 the Chinese outside attacked the Belgian legation and the Methodist Mission, both outside the defense perimeter, and burned them to the ground. Chinese troops kept up a rain of gunfire, but it was largely ineffective. That night the Chinese set fire to a house behind the British legation, hoping that the flames would spread and burn out the foreigners. But the foreigners rushed to the scene and put out the fire after two hours of fighting. The Austrians, Italians, Germans and Japanese were forced to leave their legations that night and retreat to the British legation. The Austrian and Italian legations were lost that night, but the Germans and Japanese counterattacked and returned to their legations.

Boxers on the north managed to set a fire just outside the north wall of the British compound, again hoping it would spread across the wall. They did fire the Hanlin library, which adjoined the legation on the north, separated by a narrow courtyard. To prevent the spread of the fire the foreigners tore down one building adjoining the library, then built up a barricade of sandbags and mounted a strong guard. The Boxers and Chinese Imperial troops here had come very close to breaching the barricades.

The next day the customs compound was burned by the Boxers. This building was on Customs Street, north of the French legation and across from the palace of Prince Su Wang-fu. The Austrian legation was burned, too, and the back of the Russo-Japanese bank. That night Boxers invaded a house behind the Hotel de Pekin and set it afire. Two Boxers were captured and imprisoned in the British legation.

On June 24, just after midnight, the Chinese seemed ready to launch an all-out attack. They began firing wildly at the legation quarter from every direction, but after twenty minutes of noise, without much damage, they backed off.

That day there was little fighting, except for occasional shells fired by the enemy. The Americans and the Germans moved to the Tartar wall, to try to gain holds on the wall itself and thus keep the Chinese from mounting guns that could do serious damage to the foreign compounds. The Americans took a Colt machine gun to the position and engaged in a hard fight with the Chinese. They killed a number of the enemy with the machine gun when the Chinese attacked across an open field, but then the Chinese gunners began firing on the American position and the Americans were forced to retreat back to the British legation. A few soldiers were wounded that day, mostly by snipers.

On June 25 one of the two Boxer prisoners tried to escape from the British compound so both of them were shot. That same day a message was put up on the north bridge, apparently from the Tsungli Yamen, promising the foreigners protection if they would stop shooting. The message also promised that a further message would be sent. But it never was, and a short time after the message was seen the firing began again from the Chinese lines. The foreigners took the position that this was an attempt to lure them out into the open so they could be massacred.

The Americans and the Germans moved back to the Tartar wall that afternoon and began building barricades of sandbags, under the snout of a big Chinese gun. Otherwise, it was very quiet until nightfall, and then the Chinese began firing, not so much to hit anything as to frighten the foreigners. They shot off a number of rockets that night, too, for no conceivable reason.

Inside the legation quarter the foreigners had plenty of food, thanks to the efforts of Herbert G. Squiers, first secretary of the American legation. Squiers was a sensible man who had seen the trouble coming long before either his superior, Minister Conger, or the British minister, Sir Claude MacDonald. The British minister had been particularly insensible to the changing climate in Peking, and even on the first night of the siege, when his legation was filled with hundreds of homeless foreigners and Chinese, he was seen in the courtyard in a full-dress suit. Nor was there a single sandbag or attempt at self-protection in the British compound on that first night.

There would not have been much food either, had Herbert Squiers not taken strong action. For several days he had been buying all the available wagons in Peking and had laid in huge stores of rice and other edibles. These had been brought into the legation quarter and stored in warehouses, or go-downs. When the Chinese attacked, Dr. Coltman brought several Chinese servants to the legation and helped Squiers transfer much of the food into the British legation, just in case the Chinese breached the barricades on Legation Street.

In spite of the barricades built on the Tartar wall, the position of the Americans there was tenuous. On June 26 Marine Sergeant Fanning was killed by a Chinese sniper and several other Americans and Germans were wounded. A crowd of Boxers in their red sashes, waving swords and spears, attacked the wall, but when the Americans turned the Colt machine gun on them and killed or wounded about fifty Boxers, the rest turned back.

The walls were quiet for two days. Then, on June 29 the Chinese attacked from the west, hitting toward the stables, which represented the weakest point of defense in the legation compound. These stables were located just south of the British legation, and an open passageway led to the legation. This had been barricaded, but the barricade was makeshift, and it had to be guarded at all times. About fifty British marines were guarding the area on the morning of June 29 when it was attacked by the Chinese troops. They repelled the attack, then went over the barricades with bayonets and chased the Chinese back through the Chinese houses south of the Imperial Carriage Park. They killed a number of Chinese, and captured a number of Mauser rifles and carbines and six hundred rounds of ammunition. The guns were distributed among the unarmed civilians in the legation and some of the civilians were taught to use them.

Later that day fifty British volunteers under Marine Captain Wray went out into the city to find a Chinese gun that was too close to the legation quarter. It was on the Su Wang-fu Palace grounds, across the canal from the British legation. The volunteers did not find the gun, but they did route some snipers who had taken refuge in the Chinese houses near the legation quarter. Other snipers had entered ruins near the American legation — the ruins caused by Chinese attempts to set fire to the legation in the first few hours of the siege.

On June 30 came the first rainstorm of the rainy season, and as the lightning flashed and the thunder roared, so did the Chinese guns, in what for a time seemed to be a barrage leading up to a night attack. When the storm ended, however, so did the Chinese firing, and the rest of the night was quiet.

On the south, at the Tartar wall, the Chinese began building a barricade opposite the American position, in an obvious attempt to build so high that they could look down on the wall and fire at the men behind it. This barricade became a definite threat on July 2. Soon the Americans would have to decide whether to rush the Chinese and try to capture their barricade, or leave the wall as indefensible. They could not do the latter, in the interests of the safety of the legation quarter, so they planned a night attack which would allow them to cross the forty yards that separated the two positions with the greatest chance of surprising the enemy.

At three o'clock on the morning of July 3, fifteen American marines, fifteen Russian sailors and twenty-five British marines crept over the American barricade. They divided into two parties and moved up to the face of the Chinese barricade quietly, so quietly that they were not detected. When they reached the barricade, each man let out a war whoop and rushed over the wall, or around it, shouting and firing his weapon.

The Chinese were taken completely by surprise and after a brief surge of resistance they fled. The allies counted their casualties. Two American marines had been killed. A British marine corporal was shot in the foot and British Marine Captain John Myers was wounded in the leg by a spear.

Fighting continued heatedly during the next few days, with several casualties, including the death of David Oliphant, a British student, who was shot in the compound north of the British legation. On July 6 another attempt was made to capture the gun hidden on the Su Wang-fu Palace grounds, but three Japanese soldiers were wounded in the attempt, and it had to be abandoned.

By this time, a month after the first uneasiness had been shown, the foreigners in the compound were growing worried about their chances of survival. On the night of July 6 a Chinese volunteer messenger was let down by ropes from the Tartar wall, with instructions to try to get through to Tientsin with dispatches from the diplomats that told of their situation. A number of other messengers had been sent out, through the Water Gate across the canal and over the wall, but none of them had succeeded in eluding the Chinese troops and Boxers who surrounded the legation quarter. This messenger was promised a thousand taels if he could get safely through the lines and deliver the messages. The defenders had cause to worry: The next day two attacks were launched against the French legation and Austrian Captain von Thoreburg was shot through the heart.

The foreigners had plenty of rifles and a good deal of rifle ammunition but they did not have enough of the bigger guns, including fieldpieces, with which to reply to the Chinese shelling. The Russians had brought some cannon shells up with them from Tientsin but they had not brought the gun they fit, because it had been expected that a larger force would come up within a few days after they left. Now the defenders decided to improvise. They found an old 1860 British muzzle-loading cannon which, with some adaptation, could be made to fire the shells. They fitted wheels to it from an Italian ammunition truck, and an American gunner put it all together. So they called the gun International and put it into position to knock down some of the Chinese barricades.

There were other improvisations. When the ammunition for the Italian one-pound gun ran short, the defenders scoured the Chinese houses in the area and gathered all

The old cannon in the British Legation in Peking.

the pewter vessels they could find (pewter being a common Chinese cooking and serving-dish material). The used shells were reloaded with slugs made from pewter, and revolver cartridges were used as primers.

At first there was some mutton and beef to eat, but these soon ran out and the defenders began eating horse and mule meat. First they tried the liver, and when that proved palatable they began serving other pieces in curry sauce, and finally they made sausages of horsemeat. Each adult was allowed a pound of horsemeat a day.

From prisoners captured during the first week of July the defenders learned that the troops lined up against them south of the Tartar wall were the Kansu troops of General Tung Fu-hsiang, and that General Jung Lu was in charge of another body of troops stationed behind the French legation. These would be the focal points of any attack. They also learned that the Empress had forbidden the use of large fieldpieces against the foreigners, over the objections of some of her military men, because she did not want the city to be destroyed. And finally, they learned the rumor from the prisoners that foreign troops had captured the Taku forts and occupied the Tangku railroad station. That last was the best news they had received since the cutting of the rail and telegraph lines a month earlier.

The foreigners did not understand why the Chinese did not attack them in force, but one of the prisoners gave them some indications of the reason. Since the Chinese surrounded the foreign section of the city, shots that were fired into Legation Street often went whistling out the other side, striking or threatening soldiers who did not know where the shots came from. The impression created was that the foreigners had a strong military force behind the walls, far stronger than it was. One Chinese soldier said the force was estimated to be 2,000 men with arms.

On July 13 the Chinese blew in one wall of the French legation, making it untenable, and a party of 200 Chinese troops broke through the barricades and began charging down Legation Street. They reached the bridge across the canal, although they were fired upon from the German legation. They were ready to cross the bridge and attack the United States legation when they were spotted by an American marine who gave the alarm. A dozen volleys were fired on the Chinese, killing about thirty of them. The rest turned and fled back down the street, but were caught in cross fire from the German legation, and were forced into the tennis courts of the Peking Club, behind the legation. There, eighteen more Chinese were killed, including their officer, before the rest of the group escaped over the barricades into the Chinese houses east of the club.

Two days later a messenger came into the British legation, carrying a letter from Prince Ching and other officials of the Tsungli Yamen. The prince said that he lamented the state of affairs that existed, but that the foreigners kept attacking the Chinese and so nothing could be done. He informed the foreigners that the Seymour expedition had been forced back by the Boxers. There were now so many Boxers on the Tientsin-Peking road that no one could protect the foreigners if they left Peking, the prince added. The only thing for the foreigners to do was to take their families and move out into the Tsungli Yamen itself, where, the prince said, they would be protected. No foreign troops could carry arms, of course. The foreigners were given until noon the next day to reply. "If no reply is received by the hour fixed, even our affection will not enable us to help you," said the prince.

The foreigners did not believe this message came from Prince Ching at all, but that it was a ruse by Tung Fu-hsiang or the Boxers to bring them out so they could be killed. They refused to leave the legations, and so informed the Chinese.

Actually the message had been sincere. On July 14, when it was prepared, Tientsin had fallen to the Western troops and thirteen viceroys of the Empire in the south and west of China had sent letters to the throne indicating their displeasure with the fighting. Further, the court was beginning to understand that the Boxers threatened to get out of hand. Prince Chuang had some 30,000 Boxers under his command, and most of those were in Peking. Prince Tuan claimed the allegiance of 1,400 bands of Boxers – each boasting that it had 100 to 300 men – which meant somewhere between 140,000 and 400,000 more Boxers. It was hard to tell how many Boxers there were because anyone who wanted to wear something red could claim to be a Boxer. The problem now was that they were roaming the city, robbing and looting anyone they suspected of being a Christian, and even mistreating officials. Chen Hsueh-fen, the vice president of the board of civil service, was beaten up in his office, and the newly appointed governor of Kweichow province was dragged from his sedan chair and robbed of all his clothes. The Dowager Empress was becoming disgusted with the Boxers, because they were proving themselves to be brigands and not anti-foreign patriots.

When the foreigners refused to come out of their legation area, the Tsungli Yamen announced that it would do all it could to protect them, and to show its goodwill it would demand a cessation of attacks for twelve days. On July 20, also, the Tsungli Yamen sent into the legations four cartloads of vegetables and four of watermelons.

A messenger sent out by the Japanese minister on June 30 managed to make his way back inside the foreign settlement during the truce, and he had much to report. He said that a mixed foreign force of 33,000 troops would soon set out from Tientsin to relieve the capital. He told the tale of his trip to Tientsin, and how he had made his way to the Chinese lines and waited until the city fell to the foreigners before trying to deliver his messages.

Meanwhile, the Tsungli Yamen officials became insistent that some solution to the problems of the foreigners be reached. They suggested that if the foreign ministers would not move to the Tsungli Yamen, they move to Tientsin. The Chinese army would send them by way of Tungchou and then by boat downstream, direct to Tientsin, a voyage of two days. They would be completely protected at all times.

At this time, history shows, the intentions of the Chinese government were sincere, although they had not always been so. The reason was that the Chinese knew of the coming of the foreign force, and the reasonable Chinese hoped that by getting the ministers and their families to leave Peking they could avoid the march of foreign troops on the city.

The foreigners simply would not believe the Chinese officials at this point, and so negotiations broke down. Immediately, the situation changed for the worse when a trusted old official named Li Ping-heng arrived in Peking from the Yangtze valley. Li was a patriotic man and a loyal supporter of the Manchu Empire. He was also opposed to railroads, paper money, mining, post offices and modern schools. He hated everything foreign.

Li Ping-heng arrived at Peking on July 26, 1900, after an arduous journey by way of Shantung province. He was met by Hsu T'ung and Kang I, two of the most reactionary of the Dowager Empress's advisers. He discussed the situation with them and they all agreed that the war must be carried against the foreign devils and won, so there would be a basis for negotiation on favorable ground.

As soon as Li arrived he was appointed deputy commander of the northern armies. When the news came out, the Boxers were very much encouraged, and more of them began to move into Peking. In the next few days five of the Empress's close advisers were executed, and those who advocated making peace were immediately silenced. All five of the executed officials had been advocates of peace.

Yuan Ch'ang, the first to be executed, had been the first man to speak out against the Boxers in the Imperial Council.

The second, Hsu Ching-ch'eng, had told the Dowager Empress that the Boxers should be suppressed and the foreign diplomats protected. He had tried to negotiate with the foreigners.

The third, Li Shan, had pointed out to the Dowager Empress that the Boxers were not invulnerable to foreign weapons, as they claimed to be.

The fourth, Lien Yuan, had argued before the Dowager Empress that the support of the Boxers was useless because they were little better than bandits.

The fifth, Hsu Yung I, had suggested that the murder of Baron von Ketteler was an evil act and that Prince Ching must do something about it.

Three of these men, Hsu Yung I, Li and Lien, had tried to negotiate with British Minister MacDonald.

And so they were beheaded, by order of the Dowager Empress, on July 29.

Immediately the position of the foreigners took a turn for the worse. On the very day of the executions, July 29, Li Ping-heng began building a barricade on the north bridge, and a group of Boxers took refuge behind it and started sniping at the foreigners.

7 | INCIDENTS OF THE SIEGE

If the foreigners in Peking and other parts of China were in danger, their danger was no worse than that of the Chinese Christians, for the Christians represented exactly what the Boxers wanted to eliminate: foreign influence on China. The Boxers were determined to kill the Christian Chinese, and they harried and tracked them down for that purpose.

Ch'en Ta-yung, a gatekeeper by occupation, had become a Christian and had become a preacher a few years before the Boxers arose in 1900. He had become affiliated with the Methodist Mission in Peking. When an opportunity for advancement occurred in the spring of 1900, he was given his chance to become an independent Christian pastor. On June 5 he had left Peking, taking his wife and his young son and daughter to Yen Ch'ing Chou, a town in Mongolia, outside the Great Wall of China.

Scarcely had Ch'en arrived in his new pastorate when the Boxers began causing trouble in Shantung and Chihli, and he was warned to flee to the mountains. He refused to leave until all his Christian parishioners were safe. Then he left for a hiding place in the mountains, but was observed by a member of the Boxer organization, and the Boxers pursued the family and caught them.

First the Boxers robbed the family and took their extra clothing and bedding. Then they beheaded Ch'en Ta-yung and his young son. And finally they turned to the wife and daughter and hacked them to pieces.

Such cold-blooded murders were common throughout North China. The lives of the Chinese Christians were not worth a single cash (less than a penny) if the Boxers caught them. There were many narrow escapes. The Reverend Te Jui of Shanhaikuan had a number of such escapes during the uprising. Te Jui was the presiding elder of the Shanhaikuan district, which meant he was the leading native Christian minister. On June 3, when the North China Conference of the Methodist Episcopal Church was held in Peking, the Boxers spread a rumor that they were going to attack the conference and kill all the Christian Chinese and the missionaries. They did not do so, but during the conference the meeting was told of the murders of Christians throughout the land. Afterward, Te Jui hired several carts, intending to take his party to the rail line and then return home. But the railroad between Peking and Tientsin was cut by this time, and so they tried to travel by road, planning to stop at inns along the way. Soon they learned that they were in grave danger, and returned to the Methodist Mission compound.

In Peking, on every street corner people were talking about the killing of all the foreigners and Chinese Christians. Te Jui decided that Peking was too dangerous a place to stay, so he began travelling to T'ang Shan by cart, hoping there to get a train to Shanhaikuan. It was yet only mid-June, but the Boxer tide was rising fast. On the road Te Jui discovered that all the inns were filled with Boxers and Imperial troops, and he spent his nights hiding in cemeteries. He reached Shanhaikuan safely, but ten days later the Boxers arrived there in force, led by a local tinsmith named Tuan Yi-li. They harangued the people for many hours on the streets, and persuaded about 800 Manchu soldiers in the area to join under their red banner. They intended to burn the Christian chapel, they said.

Te Jui went to see the local magistrate, the highest official in Shanhaikuan, and asked for help. The magistrate was a kindly man and was well-disposed toward the Christians. He said he would turn the chapel into a police station in order to protect it. Two days later the Boxers came to the chapel at noon, shouting that they intended to burn it down and kill the Christians.

The Boxers came to the chapel on June 20, but were turned away by the police inside. Two days later the magistrate, who had gone to Peking on affairs of government, returned with the startling news that Baron von Ketteler had been killed and that the foreigners of Peking were besieged in the legation area and in the missions.. The magistrate advised Te Jui to close his chapel and flee while he could still be saved. If the foreigners conquered China the chapel could be returned to him, but if the Boxers won, all the Christians would be put to death, the magistrate said.

Te Jui hid in the home of a church member outside the Great Wall, to await developments. One of his Christians, a man named Wang P'u, was captured by the Boxers, and a few days later they killed him along with two other Christians. By this time Te Jui had seen enough and he fled to Neuyangkou, a village seventeen miles from Shanhaikuan, to hide with a Christian family. He learned that his chapel had been burned four days after the murder of Wang P'u.

The people of Shanhaikuan soon learned of Te Jui's whereabouts and a party of Boxers came after him. He fled from one Christian house to another, from one village to the next, sometimes staying one night, sometimes staying as long as three nights, but always moving on.

In Shanhaikuan the Boxers offered a reward of 100 ounces of silver for Te Jui or his head. The Boxers pursued him relentlessly and he was forced to separate from his wife and family lest they all be captured together. With another Christian pastor, Tseng Kuo-chih, Te Jui set out for Ch'ouyang, which was outside the Great Wall and where they hoped to find safety. They travelled in the common blue cloth pajamas of the peasants, wearing coolie straw hats. They buried their own clothing beside the road so it would not be found.

Every village through which they passed was filled with Boxers, so many that eventually they turned back toward Shanhaikuan because there was no safety outside the wall. They planned to go to the home of a local Christian just outside Shanhaikuan, but when they were recognized by an acquaintance of Tseng's they were warned that the Boxers were watching that place. They hid in a cave for two days without food or water. They decided to go and hide in the North Mountains, but did not know the way. They set out for Chin Men Kuan, but were warned that the Imperial soldiers were guarding the gate of that town and would stop them. They went by a rocky mountain path instead, afraid to approach a spring or a house, suffering from thirst and hunger all the way. They passed by a Christian graveyard and saw a number of men there, but were not noticed. Later they discovered that these men were Boxers desecrating the Christian graves.

They moved quietly, hiding when necessary and endangering themselves every time they spoke to a stranger, for they might be unmasked as Christians and turned over to the Boxers. They were protected for a time by a herdsman named Li Chu who fed them and found them a cave in which to live. For a month they slept in the cave or in Li Chu's house at night and hid in the kaoliang fields in the daytime. Eventually they started for Lanchow and made their way along the roads through crowds of Boxers to that city.

Not only Christians, but anyone who had anything to do with the foreigners was in danger. Boxers roamed the streets of the cities and the roads of the villages, carrying long knives and spears, ready to murder any they suspected. Several hundred students at Peking University were among those threatened, because they were Christians and because they were learning foreign ways.

When the troubles began the students met with missionaries and decided what they should do. Some students went home to their villages to escape the danger. Others remained in Peking in the mission compound. They began digging trenches around the college buildings. But it was not long before the order came for the Chinese Christian students to go to the British legation, and they went. They arrived in Legation Street and were stopped for half an hour at the Italian legation while the defenders decided what would be done with these Chinese Christians.

Eventually they were taken to the Su Wang-fu Palace, and told to stay there while quarters were made available. They remained in the hot sun at the Su Wang-fu for several hours.

All this occurred on June 20, the day Baron von Ketteler was murdered and the siege really began. In the middle of the afternoon the men students found one of the shops open in the legation quarter and took rice and flour. If the Western powers came to rescue the Christians, the shopkeeper would be paid, they told him. If they did not, he too would most probably be killed by the Boxers. The shopkeeper agreed and gave them what they wanted.

On June 21 the students formed a committee of eight members – four Protestant and four Catholic – to provide various services within the community. They established organizations for defense, provisions, sanitation and general labor. They built sandbag barricades and defended the Su Wang-fu Palace for a week. By the end of the first week, however, the Su was under such heavy fire from Boxers and Chinese soldiers that the civilians were evacuated and the area was left in the hands of Japanese soldiers and some students-turned-soldiers.

There were strange occurrences and some that humiliated the Chinese. Professor Lu, chairman of the university committee, was ordered by a French soldier to do coolie work and it was not until a Chinese- and English-speaking Frenchman was found that the soldier learned his mistake in threatening a man of such dignity. Two other teachers were put in charge of coolies and one was made a messenger boy. Here is one student's account of the life they led:

> Those of us who worked in the trenches suffered many hardships, having to work in a pouring rain or a

scorching sun, often up to our knees in mud, with nothing to eat but a bowl of fermented rice, and not infrequently we were called out at night to help fight the fire.

But those of us who were at work on the barricades were in more immediate danger from the bullets of the enemy. We realized that for the safety of all it was necessary that the lives of the foreigners be preserved, so that we often occupied without hesitation the most exposed positions in barricade-building rather than allow our foreign leaders to do so. In spite of this but one of our number was killed while carrying bricks, though many were wounded. Often our hearts almost failed us as we ran through the exposed places to build up the barricades or stood filling sandbags while the shot fell like hail all around us, with an occasional shell or cannon ball whizzing overhead or striking the wall we were building.

The danger to which those who were messenger boys was exposed was equally great, for no matter how thick the shot and shell were falling they were compelled to go from legation to legation, indeed when the danger was greatest their services were most in demand. One traversing the streets was especially exposed. This was particularly true in crossing the Legation Street bridge, where he was an open target from four directions. Often they would wait until there was a lull in the firing and then cross with a rush, not infrequently with the cannon balls or bullets whizzing past their ears or over their heads.

Even in this danger the Chinese were not treated as

equals by the foreigners. When a mule was killed for the foreigners to eat, each foreigner received a pound of mule meat each day. The Chinese students got no more than a single cup of fermented rice, and as for the mule meat, they received the entrails and the head and feet, and that was all.

They displayed no particular resentment, however, because they were used to the discriminations of the foreigners.

The students played a brave part in the defense of the legations. One night a man who had formerly been a Buddhist priest put on Buddhist clothing and went out to try to buy copies of the *Peking Gazette*. He was caught by the Boxers but was released when he convinced them that he was a Buddhist and not a Christian.

Students who had returned home instead of coming to the legation area were in constant danger from the Boxers. One student went home, discovered the danger into which he was placing himself and all the members of his family, and fled at night to the mountains. The Boxers followed him and he kept going, until he was 250 miles from home. Here he put up at an inn, only to have a Boxer chief come into the inn and inspect the guests, to determine if there were any Christians among them.

The Boxer chief ordered the people at the inn to take off their caps. Then he rubbed their foreheads between eyes and nose to see if there was a cross on the forehead, for the Boxers believed that all Christians wore crosses on their foreheads. That was why, they said, the foreigners all wore hats pulled tightly down on their heads.

The students became the messengers who tried to get through to Tientsin, too. The Japanese were the first to send a messenger through the lines, and their messenger was a student named Cheng Tien-fang. One day shortly after the siege began the Japanese minister came to the Su Wang-fu and asked for a messenger. Cheng said he was willing to try to make it to Tientsin, and he was promised 1,000 taels (1,000 ounces of silver) if he could make it safely and return. He said he would do it, but not for money, and the next day he received the message from the Japanese minister.

Cheng sewed the letter into the heel of his shoe and set out for Peking.

"I had hardly left the defenses," he said, "when a bullet whistled close to my head. I ran a few steps, being rather frightened. Just then I saw a number of people going along the street carrying bundles of things they had looted from burning buildings, and I mingled with the crowd, going north past the Temple of Imperial Ancestors, where the decaying bodies of the dead, piled one upon the other, were so offensive as to compel me to hold my nose."

He went to the spot where Baron von Ketteler had been killed, and found all the stores closed and sealed on that street. He went to the east gate of the city and discovered the streets were lined with tents and soldiers, and the gates were guarded by Boxers.

The first day Cheng Tien-fang made his way to Tung-chou and took a boat down river toward Tientsin, through crowds of Boxers, who kept boarding the boat to see if there were any Christians trying to escape. After three days Cheng arrived at the red bridge in Tientsin. But when he tried to enter the city he discovered it was surrounded by Chinese soldiers and he could not pass. He put up at a small inn near the bridge for several days, trying one side of the city and then another, but he could not get through the Chinese lines.

On July 14 he went to Ch'en Chia Kou, where a battle was being fought between Chinese and foreigners, and he saw the dead Chinese so thick they seemed to be piled on top of one another. He went back to his inn each night, and each morning went out to try to find a way into the city. At noon on July 16 he went out in the intense heat, when the Chinese troops near the railroad station retired to their tents to escape the heat. Foreign soldiers began firing at him, and nearly hit him, but he waved a white handkerchief and they allowed him to enter the station area. He had found the Japanese troops who were guarding the platform.

The troops sent Cheng to the Japanese consul, and Cheng showed him on a map where the concentrations of Chinese troops were, as well as he could recall. The consul then took the information and the letter to the allied commanders, and gave Cheng another letter and $10 for expenses.

Cheng sewed the letter inside his shoe again and set out for Peking. He was stopped by Russian soldiers when he tried to pass through the lines, and had to return to the Japanese consulate for assistance. The consul sent soldiers to accompany him to the lines, and they did so. Hardly had they gone out of his sight when he was arrested by Chinese soldiers who accused him of being a messenger for the Westerners. They stripped him and searched all his clothing except his shoes, and then let him go, convinced that he had nothing of value.

He returned to Tungchou by boat. Outside Peking he took the precaution of having his head shaved in the

Buddhist fashion before returning to the city. He returned to find people carrying food into the legation quarter (this was during the twelve-day truce) and he mingled with the crowd and made his way into the Japanese legation, to deliver the first word that the allied powers were sending a relief expedition to Peking. The Japanese minister was as good as his word, and Cheng received his 1,000 taels. He meant what he had said about not wanting money, for he used half the 1,000 taels to found a scholarship for poor boys at Peking University.

Another student messenger who set out to carry letters from the besieged legation quarter to Tientsin was Yao Chen-yuan, who used another technique for concealing his letters. He sewed them into a large straw hat of the kind used by coolies. The hat consisted of two layers, so he pulled them apart and put the letters between the layers.

Yao set out from the Su Wang-fu and was immediately stopped by two Japanese soldiers. They asked where he was going and when he told them that he was carrying letters they warned him to be careful and escorted him to the edge of Legation Street, near the barricade. He went on alone then past a Boxer who collected ten cents for letting him pass, and out the city gate toward Tungchou. He was overtaken on the road by 300 of Tung Fu-hsiang's soldiers, but they did not bother him. Indeed, when they came to a canal that had overflowed its banks and created a great lake, one of the soldiers swam with Yao on his back to the other side.

Yao and several of the soldiers stayed that first night at an inn. He was accosted by a woman Boxer chief who said she was a member of the Society of the Red Lantern. She asked his name, his business and his destination and he made up a story that seemed to satisfy her. The next morning he was befriended by another Boxer, who bought his breakfast and went with him part of the way to Tungchou.

On the road Yao saw many atrocities. He saw twenty people burned in one village because the Boxers suspected they might be Christians. He was stopped many times and asked the same question: Who was he and where was he going? He gave the same answer — he was Yao Chen-yuan and he was going to Tientsin to try to find the head of a landscape garden where he had worked before the troubles began.

It was an odd enough and specific enough answer to satisfy anyone — and it was partly true because Yao had been a landscape gardener before he became a Christian student.

Yao was robbed by a band of soldiers, but their officer came along and returned his money and gave him protection for the night. He also warned Yao not to fall into the hands of the foreign soldiers because they would surely kill him. Yao agreed with all the officer said, and went on his way, trying to find the foreigners.

He found a boatman who agreed to take him to the red bridge that led to Tiensin, and he had no difficulty at all, because when he reached the bridge he was met by Japanese soldiers who did not shoot at him, but escorted him to the city. There he was stopped by the Russians, who would not let him pass until a Japanese officer came along and, when Yao showed him the letters, took him to his headquarters. Later that day Yao was taken to the American consul.

Yao remained in Tientsin for two days, and then began

the return trip with letters for the besieged foreigners in Peking. He was robbed again, this time by two foreign soldiers. Again an officer came to his rescue and forced the men to return the money.

Seven miles outside Tientsin, Yao encountered a band of Boxers but after he told them the story about the landscape gardener they let him alone. He encountered many more bands of Boxers on the trip back to Peking, but in each case he faced them boldly and they did not seem to suspect that he was anything other than he said he was.

When he came to the city wall outside the east gate, Yao stopped at a noodle stand and ate two bowls of noodles, all the while watching the soldiers and Boxers on top of the city wall. He entered the city and began walking slowly toward the legation quarter, sauntering along so that it would look as though he were going nowhere. It took him from noon until dusk to reach the legation area. There, between the Chinese barricades and the foreigners' barricades, he encountered a Chinese soldier.

"Hello! Captain, what are you doing?" Yao asked.

"What are *you* doing here?" the soldier asked.

"Please do not speak so loud," said Yao in a conspiratorial voice. "I was originally a coolie in this place. My home is in the country and I have just been to see if my family were killed, and finding them safe I have returned to get some treasure I have in the Su Wang-fu."

"How much have you?"

"About one thousand dollars," Yao replied.

"What is your name?" asked the soldier.

"Yao Chen-yuan. What is your honorable name?"

"Wu Lien-t'ai," said the soldier. "Now you go and get your silver and we two will open an opium shop."

Yao and the soldier continued to talk. The soldier asked for money, and Yao gave him all the silver he had with him. The soldier promised to return it when Yao came back with his 1,000 taels. Just then an officer came up with about 50 soldiers, and when he saw Yao in the area he became very suspicious and talked loudly of having him killed.

"Do not kill him," said the soldier. "He is an old friend of mine from the country, here to make money out of the foreigners."

"If he is a friend of yours," said the officer suspiciously, "what is his name?"

"Yao Chen-yuan," the soldier said easily.

"What is this soldier's name?" the officer asked Yao.

"Wu Lien-t'ai," Yao answered promptly.

The officer was satisfied and Yao might have gone into the foreign compounds then, but as they were talking a group of Boxers came up and asked what Yao was doing in the area, for innocent civilians kept far away from the perimeter of the foreigners' part of the city these days. Wu Lien-t'ai told the Boxers to go away and mind their own business and he escorted Yao to the wall. The Japanese soldiers who had stopped Yao many days earlier recognized him and helped him over the wall. He went to see Secretary Squiers at the American legation and delivered to him no fewer than 11 letters. His had been a most successful adventure.

Not all the Christian Chinese were so lucky as Yao and Cheng. Many hundreds and thousands who were not even helping the foreigners were killed by the Boxers simply because they had taken the foreign religion and foreign ways. Among these was Wang Chih-shien, one of the brightest students in the senior class of Peking University that year. Wang had gone home just before the Boxer Rebellion began, and the local Boxer group in his home town came to him and insisted that he either recant his faith in Christianity or die. He chose death and urged repentence on his captors with such fervor that they cut off his lips to stop his talk. Then they cut off his arms and legs and finally they hacked the still-living torso to death.

Dr. Wang Chung-lin was a Christian and a medical doctor who was associated with Peking University. When the Boxers began to grow active in Chihli province, Wang sent his wife and children to his father's home in the country, but remained in Peking himself. He did not even go into the legation sector of Peking when the trouble began, and he was among several hundred students and teachers who were massacred around the college in the first days of the struggle. He had been offered a chance to recant, but he had refused, so the Boxers stabbed him with spears and threw his body under the college building.

A girl named Hsu Hui-fang suffered a particularly horrible fate at the hands of the Boxers. She was a teacher at a girls' school at Tsunhua, and when the Boxers descended on the school she fled to the mountains. A band of Boxers followed her and she was shot in the face by a Chinese matchlock. She survived the wound. Several times she was offered her freedom and her life if she would become the concubine of a Boxer leader. She refused. She was taken to Pingancheng to be beheaded in public. The executioner's sword broke as it struck her neck. The Boxers then rushed in with knives and spears, cut her body to pieces and then burned it.

8 | THE FALL OF PEKING

After the capture of Tientsin on July 14 it might have been possible for the troops of the allied powers to march quickly to the relief of the Peking foreign compounds, but this was not to be the case. In fact, the senior officers in the field did not even consider such a move, for a number of reasons.

It was at first believed that the Peking foreign settlement had been massacred and plans were laid for the dispatch of a punitive force to investigate in Peking. This force was not to be sent until around September 15 because it would take that long to land and supply 60,000 troops – the number the senior officers deemed necessary to defeat the Chinese forces.

Troops were on the way: Japanese, Russian, American and 3,000 British Indian soldiers who had been called to active service on June 19 when it became apparent that there would be trouble. But the 7th Rajput Regiment, as it was known, could not leave Calcutta for a week after being alerted, and it took a little more than two weeks for two steamers to travel from Calcutta to the Taku Bar. All along the way similar difficulties were encountered by all the nations.

Before the fall of Tientsin the commanders had badly overestimated the strength of the Chinese forces. After the fall of the city they were still very unsure of themselves. They knew that the Chinese had opened the sluices of the Pei Ho, and they soon discovered that the water in the river had fallen so low that boats drawing more than four feet could not navigate upstream. That eliminated travel by foreign ship. Further, the kaoliang, the huge Chinese millet that grows twice as high as a man's head, was in full ripening, and stood everywhere across the plain that stretches between Tientsin and Peking. There were no adequate roads along which the artillery and cavalry could advance. The Chinese troops and the Boxers were entrenched in the villages along the railroad.

All these considerations were given little more than academic study during most of July because no one really believed that the legations were still intact. On July 20, however, the United States Secretary of State in Washington received a coded message from Minister Conger in Peking, which gave the allied governments their first indication of the true state of affairs there.

"For one month," said the message, "we have been besieged in British Legation under continued shot and shell from Chinese troops. Quick relief only can prevent general massacre."

This news had been transmitted during that brief respite when the advocates of peace seemed to be gaining control in the Tsungli Yamen, and with the Dowager Empress. The coded message got through before Li Ping-heng took charge and the warhawks did away with the advocates of peace.

The message was quickly sent on to Tientsin for the eyes of the allied commanders there.

On receipt of this message British General Gaselee and American General Chaffee in Tientsin insisted that an attempt to relieve Peking must be made. If the others did not wish to help, it was up to them, said the British and American generals, but they were going to take a column to Peking.

In the eyes of the Germans, Russians, Japanese and French, it would never do to allow the British and Americans to get the upper hand in China. Therefore, the argument ended immediately and provisions were made to put an army into the field.

A column of boats was formed to carry supplies by the water route up the Pei Ho. Ten days' rations and ammunition were put aboard, and some boats were used to carry engineers' supplies, while others were made into "hospital boats." The river was so low that native junks and sampans had to be used, and they were towed and poled by Chinese coolies. The boat column extended along the snaky turns of the river for six miles.

On August 4, the relief column set out from Tientsin for Peking, determined to follow the river generally, to keep the supplies within reasonable distance, but moving more quickly and directly than the supply train. The column was led by 8,000 Japanese troops under Lieutenant General Baron F. Yamaguchi, 4,500 Russians under General Linievitch, 3,000 British under General Gaselee, 2,500 Americans under General Chaffee and 800 French troops under General

British junks being towed up the Pei Ho.

Frey. The Germans did not send any forces after all, deciding it was best to concentrate their strength in Shantung province where they must protect their colony of Kiaochow.

Each officer and man was given two days' rations and on the afternoon of August 4, behind a fife and drum band, the foreigners marched through the native city of Tientsin to a point about four miles outside the city, where they were caught in a heavy rainstorm and decided to bivouac for the night.

General Sung Ching, the Commander-in-Chief who fought the battle of Tientsin against the allied forces.

Scouts had discovered that a strong Chinese force under General Sung Ch'ing was holding the town of Peich'ang, which lay astride the Pei Ho a few miles ahead. The allies needed control of the river or they could not progress, so the time for the first battle had come. It was to be a night attack, led by the Japanese, who would move out at one o'clock in the morning, with other troops scheduled to take the flanks and keep the rearguard.

The Chinese force was estimated at 25,000, but the foreigners believed that with superior weapons and their better trained troops they would be able to defeat General Sung. Still the weather was difficult, for it rained all night.

At one o'clock in the morning the barrage began and the first Japanese troops moved out, meeting the advance Chinese guard at a point about two miles north of Hsi Ku. With the other troops on their flanks the Japanese bore the brunt of the attack, moving into heavy and accurate Chinese cannon fire. Japanese guns, and the guns of the British Royal Field Artillery's No. 12 battery and the Hong Kong and Singapore Artillery moved to cover a point at a bend in the Pei Ho called Nansung, where the Chinese had determined to make a stand. The Japanese troops moved up under cover of these guns to the Chinese trenches with the British First Bengal Lancers on their right. The Japanese suffered most severely, losing about 300 men killed and wounded in the heavy fighting. But by noon the Chinese had disappeared from the right bank of the river and were fleeing north along the left bank.

After the victory, the allies pushed ahead for two miles along the right bank but were stopped by floods. The Chinese had opened the sluices in the river's retaining walls and had flooded the right side of the river. Between floods and the almost impenetrable kaoliang, the allies were forced to move back to the Nansung position and cross the river. So the Chinese army had a chance to escape and move to another prepared position.

There was little time to be lost. The allies moved quickly on August 6. The Japanese moved up the river along the left bank, and after the flooded areas had been passed the British, French, Russians and Americans moved up the right bank. It was hard going because the road along the left bank was so badly rutted and pitted. The British artillery was forced to move its guns into junks, which took much time and put them out of action. They were towed up to Tungchou, finally, being taken off the junks when it was necessary to bring them into action.

The British troops led the advance up the right bank, the Russians and French following and the Americans deployed out to the right flank to protect against envelopment by the Chinese. As they came into sight of the town of Yangtsun they saw that the Chinese were prepared to make a stand there. At this point the railroad bridged the river, but the troops of General Sung Ch'ing had blown up the bridge and were entrenched on the right embankment of the river, ready to fight. Since the bridge was gone the Japanese could not come across from the left bank and join the action, so the fighting was to be carried by the British, French, Russians and Americans.

American troops of the 14th Infantry division began to move ahead on the right. The British moved forward in the center. The Russian infantry moved ahead on the left. British and Russian artillery stayed on the left, American artillery moved to the right. Again it was hard going as soon as the soldiers moved away from the edge of the river-

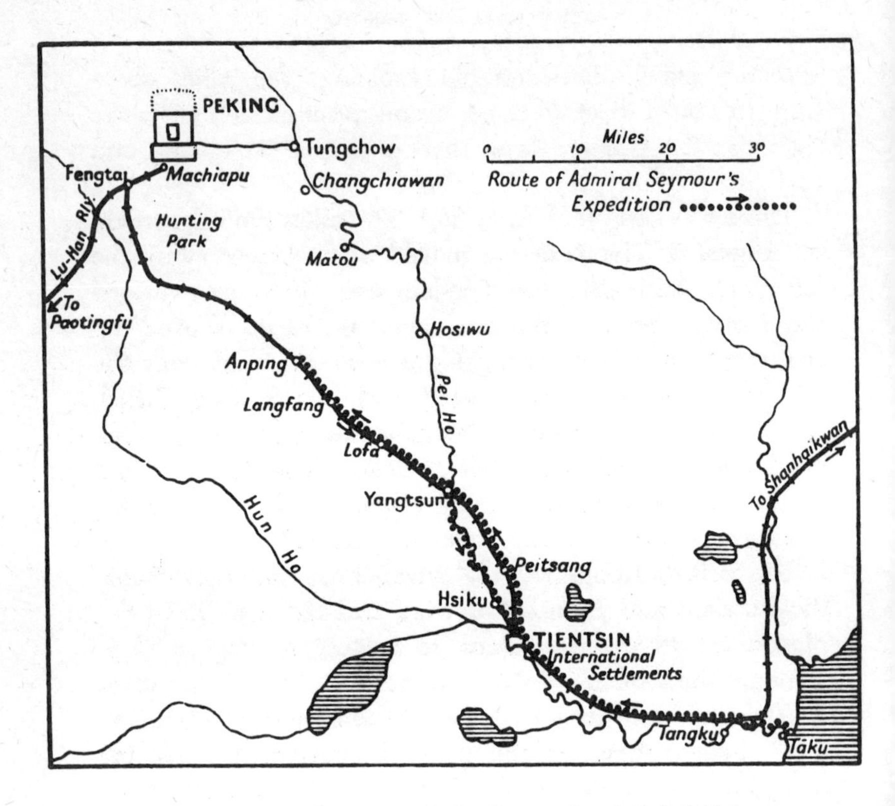

Map showing the route of the International Relief Force.

bank, because of the tall kaoliang in the flat fields. It was 5,000 yards from the point where the advance began to the Chinese position. When the infantry had advanced half that distance, the Chinese artillery began firing and the small guns and snipers opened up, too, as the allies came within range.

Around noon the Chinese were driven from their trenches and the allied troops moved in to follow them over a hill beyond the bridge and the town. Then, by mistake, allied guns in the rear opened fire on their own troops, killing and wounding a number of Americans and Sikhs. One American officer rode along directly in front of the guns, shouting at the gunners:

"Stop firing! You are killing our own men!"

Private Jackson of the Royal Welch Fusiliers got up on the railway embankment, even as the allied guns were firing into it and over it, and tried to communicate with the gunners. The Chinese opened fire on him.

It was a problem of languages and different customs. The Russian guns were calibrated in meters and the British spotters were giving their instructions in yards. At one time, too, a group of British soldiers mistook some Russian troops for Chinese and opened fire on them, so the Russians began firing back.

Eventually the entire position, bridge, town and railroad station were taken. The Russians had the hardest job, forcing the Chinese out of the railroad station and the entrance to the bridge.

At the end of the fighting, Lieutenant Colonel H. B. Vaughan of the 7th Rajput Regiment described the scene:

> While halted here and waiting for orders, I climbed up on the lofty railway embankment close by, and stood on the site of the station, which had been utterly destroyed by the Boxers; even the very foundations of the houses had been dug up. Our field battery now came up, and from this elevated position opened fire on the villages through which the enemy were retreating. Many dead Chinamen lay about. Close by was the railway bridge over the Pei Ho, an iron girder bridge

> supported on concrete piers. The Boxers had partially destroyed the pier on the farther bank, and the girder was still resting on the piers, but so displaced that trains could not cross it. Had they completely destroyed the bridge piers, letting the girders fall into the water, it is difficult to see how the boat column could have continued its advance until the removal of the obstacles. . . .

But the Chinese had not destroyed the bridge completely as they should have done, and the advance was not stopped. The Chinese commander had been thoroughly confident of victory at this point. Li Ping-heng had left Peking that very morning, to direct the rout of the foreigners and was on his way to Mat'ou. But so terrible was the disaster that the Chinese viceroy could not face the commander, and as Li came south, the viceroy committed suicide.

The allied army stopped at Yangtsun and rested on August 7, for the men were quite worn out by marching and fighting beneath the hot North China sun. Meanwhile, at noon on that day, Li Ping-heng arrived at Mat'ou and learned the extent of the disaster that had befallen his armies.

On August 8, the allied troops began marching again, except for the French, who remained behind because their baggage had not caught up with them and they were short of supplies. The Japanese were in front.

The allied troops passed through several lines of Chinese trenches, still occupied by a handful of dead bodies. Because of the intense heat the marchers were very informal. One Russian baggage train was escorted by an officer who rode in a rickshaw to which he had hitched a mule instead of a coolie. The Indian troops passed by a store of abandoned Chinese parasols and picked them up, using them to protect their heads from the blazing sun. Men of various nations exchanged equipment, so Americans wore British puttees and Britons wore American gaiters and Japanese wore Russian Manchurian hats.

The force made only ten miles that day because of the heat. When the village of Tsaitsun was reached the commanders called a halt, and the troops went into bivouac to await the arrival of the train of junks with their supplies. Two squadrons of Bengal Lancers and the Japanese cavalry were sent out as scouts, and they returned late in the afternoon to report that the Chinese outposts were no more than a mile from the allied bivouacs. The Chinese were in force at Hohsiwu, and it seemed likely that they were prepared to make a stand there. The allied commanders then laid plans for the next day's battle.

Early in the morning the Japanese moved out and advanced on Hohsiwu. A mixed cavalry brigade – Japanese, British and Russians – was formed, but the Russians refused to act under the orders of the Japanese commander. (Throughout the campaign the frictions between officers of the various armies created much confusion.) The Japanese and the British cavalry worked together on this day, however, and worked well. Two squadrons of the Bengal Lancers routed about 250 Chinese cavalrymen and 150 infantrymen in a thickly wooded area near the village, and threatened to outflank the Chinese at Hohsiwu. The Chinese retreated again without making a stand. They had prepared for it, there was no doubt about that. A large deep moat had been dug completely around the village, the kaoliang had been cut for several hundred yards out to provide a field of fire and prevent the allies from approaching under cover. But the moat had not been filled with water – the sluice gates above the town had not been opened – because the allies had approached too quickly. (Even so, the Chinese newspapers later carried a story that the moat had been completed, that the river had been breached and that 25,000 foreigners had been drowned. Obviously that was the plan, although it did not work.)

While the allies had been marching against Hohsiwu, Li Ping-heng had been bringing new forces south to join with the commander in that area, Ma Yu-k'un, and make a stand at which he hoped to defeat the foreigners decisively. But Ma had retreated again, this time to Mat'ou.

After the battle at Hohsiwu on August 9, General Yamaguchi called a halt to the march for the day. The junks with the baggage came up that afternoon, and the troops stopped to bathe in the river which was only three feet deep here, although the current was so swift that a man could not walk upstream unaided.

The heat was bothering all the troops, even the Indians who were used to intense heat. Several horses died from the heat and many soldiers dropped out of the line of march, suffering from heat exhaustion.

Tired as his troops were, General Yamaguchi pressed them on the next day. A newspaper correspondent came upon General Fukushima that day, and said that the general looked tired.

"I am," said the general, "and our troops are tired; but the enemy are more tired, and we mean to keep them so."

On August 10 the allies moved into Mat'ou and again the Chinese retreated. Li Ping-heng was in direct command at this point, but he was having a difficult time controlling his troops, as he reported to the Imperial Palace in Peking that day:

> I have retreated from Ma'tou to Changchiawan. For the past few days I have seen several tens of thousands of troops jamming all the roads. They fled as soon as they heard of the arrival of the enemy; they did not give battle at all.
>
> As they passed the villages and towns, they set fire and plundered, so much so that there was nothing left for the armies under my command to purchase, with the result that men and horses were hungry and exhausted. [In several places the allied troops came upon half-eaten horses which had been abandoned by the fleeing Chinese troops.]
>
> From youth to old age I have experienced many wars, but never saw things like these. . . .
>
> Unless we restore discipline and execute the retreating generals and escaping troops, there will be no place where we can stand, but I am unable to do this because of lack of authority. . . .

He also wrote about his commanders. One's troops were too green to fight. One general was crafty, he said, but he knew nothing about war. Two other generals were good soldiers, but they did not have enough troops.

"As all the armies are taking to flight," Li Ping-heng wrote, "the situation is getting out of control. There is no time to regroup and deploy." (This was just what General Yamaguchi intended.)

Li Ping-heng promised the Dowager Empress that he would do his best to save the situation, to collect the fleeing troops and that he would fight to the death.

On the morning of August 11 the Japanese resumed their pressure on the Chinese, and attacked Changchiawan, to which Li Ping-heng had retreated the day before. By eight o'clock in the morning it was already hot, and the troops were sweating as they marched to attack. The Russian Cossacks fell into an ambush and lost several men. They were nearly cut off altogether by Chinese cavalry in what was one of the first spirited actions launched by the Chinese. But when the mass of Japanese infantry moved in on Changchiawan, and the big guns came up to begin shelling the village, once again the Chinese retreated. Li Ping-heng had done his best, but he could not stop the rout.

Li and the demoralized Chinese forces fell back on Tungchou, a city only fifteen miles south of Peking, and Li determined to make a last stand there that same day. He was in position by noon. The Japanese might have stopped at Changchiawan, but General Yamaguchi was relentless and he sensed that he had his enemy on the run. It was only five miles from Changchiawan to Tungchou. The Japanese moved their artillery up and began to bombard the town, ready to make the infantry assault at dawn on August 12.

When the guns opened up the Chinese troops fled. And that same afternoon, as his soldiers deserted the city, Li Ping-heng kept his promise to the Dowager Empress. He took his own life, rather than face the disgrace.

9 | THE FALL OF PEKING — II

Early on the morning of August 12 the Japanese infantry led the advance into Tungchou, the upstream terminus of navigation on the Pei Ho. The allies were very surprised to learn that the Chinese troops had again fled, for this city was the last defensive point at which the troops could stand and protect Peking.

Although there was no opposition at Tungchou, the advance was halted for the day so the troops might rest and prepare themselves for the fierce struggle that was expected to take place at Peking. The British unloaded their guns from the junks, for this was as far as the junks might take them, and prepared to haul them overland. That evening the senior commanders met to lay plans for the next day.

On the morning of August 13, British, American and Russian troops moved out at dawn to reconnoiter. It was planned that the ground would be examined during this first day, on the second day the troops would move forward to the best points of attack and on the third day the assault against Peking would begin. The First Bengal Lancers, the Japanese and the Russians all sent out cavalry.

The British were to examine the roads south of the canal that connected Tungchou with Peking and to check the east gate of the city, where they had been led to believe the best point of entry could be found. The Americans were on their right and the Russians were to the right of the Americans.

It was hard going, again through the tall kaoliang, which was deep and thick as a jungle. The cavalry kept in touch because the men could see the tips of the lances of their fellows as they moved through the tall grain.

The troops passed through several villages, all of them deserted except by the very old, who sat in the sun and waited.

The British moved forward about eight miles to a large tomb where they called a halt for the night. They encountered no opposition. The Americans were about a mile away on the right, and they saw no action. But at about midnight a Cossack went riding back to Tungchou carrying a message that said the Russians had advanced right to the Peking city walls (against orders) and had managed to secure a foothold on the Tartar City's wall. They needed reinforcements.

Immediately the troops in Tungchou began to move out and march the fifteen miles to Peking. The British left at two o'clock on the morning of August 14 and advanced toward the southeast gate. Their main force bombarded a village a mile outside the city, and when there was no reply from the Chinese they headed into Peking by the Shahaomen, working through the streets of the Chinese city until they reached the middle southern gate of the

The Water Gate under the wall of the Tartar City, through which some of the allied forces entered Peking after the siege.

Tartar City, the Chienmen. They were very near the legation quarter.

General Gaselee and the British troops headed toward the Water Gate, which runs through the south wall of the Tartar City. It was near this gate that the Americans inside Peking had conducted their spirited defense of the wall during the siege.

The First Bengal Lancers led the way, heading for the Water Gate, while the Sikhs moved to the Chienmen. They were fired upon by Chinese hiding in the tower of the Hatamen, but they headed on toward the Water Gate. Lieutenant Colonel Vaughan, who was leading an element of the 7th Rajputs, described his adventure later:

Part of the wall around the Tartar City, Peking. The structure on top of the wall to the left is a fortification; the building on the wall to the right indicates the location of the Hatamen Gate.

We went on, the men keeping close under the houses on the north side of the street to cover them from fire from the city walls and from the fire from the Hatamen gate. We were now in a street separated by one row of houses only from the ditch and the walls of the city; the whole place was completely deserted. At last an opening appeared in the houses on our right, and we saw the English, American and other European flags hanging idly in folds from the flagstaffs erected on the bastions of the walls, for not a breath of air was stirring.

Our first impression was — well, all the powers have managed somehow to get into the city before us, and we felt annoyed. Then we saw a head or two appear over the battlements, and a sailor standing right up on the wall waving a signal flag. Then the low roof of the sluice gate [Water Gate] arch appeared, and the sailor lowered his flag and waved it toward it; we followed the track down into the ditch, which was flanked by the works of the Hatamen and Chienmen gates. The whole space was clear. I turned to [Lt.] Loch and said, "Why, I believe there are the legations." I shouted to the sailor, "Which way?" and he pointed again; then more heads cautiously appeared, hats were waved and the people on the ramparts began to cheer, to which we responded, and so amid the cheering we entered the cutting joining the sluice gate to the ditch and, reaching the gate, halted.

That is the tale of the relief of the legations on August 14, 1900, after eight weeks of siege. The relief column had come none too soon, because on learning of the defeats of the Chinese armies, the Boxers and the militant anti-foreigners were launching ever more powerful attacks on the legation quarter and just the night before the relief arrived had come the strongest attack of all.

It was considered a miracle that the 500 defenders of the legation quarter had been able to withstand the attacks of thousands of Boxers and Chinese troops, and the miracle was never satisfactorily explained. In an analysis of the

Boxer Rebellion published in 1955, Chester C. Tan concluded that the foreigners were saved only because there were important Chinese officials who wanted them saved. Even when the Boxers were strongest, and when the Dowager Empress urged them on against the foreigners, the leaders of the troops held back, realizing that the murder of the foreigners would cost China dear.

Mr. Tan gave credit for this to Jung Lu, one of the Empress's leading military men, and commander of many of the Imperial troops pitted against the legation. The salvation was accomplished by indirection, he said. Jung Lu did not stand up for the foreigners. He simply did not prosecute the attacks against them as vigorously as he could have. There were several occasions on which the Chinese could have overwhelmed the foreign colony – as at the beginning of the struggle, when the British legation became the central defense point but was not yet defended.

But if the rescue of the legations seemed to be terribly easy, such was not the case elsewhere in Peking. When the 24th Punjab Infantry entered Peking, they marched to the Temple of Heaven in the southern part of the Chinese city, under fire from Chinese in the buildings along the way. The south gate of the city was still held by the Chinese, and part of the 24th Punjab was sent to cut off the enemy retreat to the east, while other British troops attacked frontally. First Secretary Squiers of the American legation took a party of legation guards, when they saw the troops coming, and charged out to clear the wall between the legation area and the Chienmen, and helped the Sikhs break through the gate and into the city.

The legation quarter was well-cleared in an hour or so

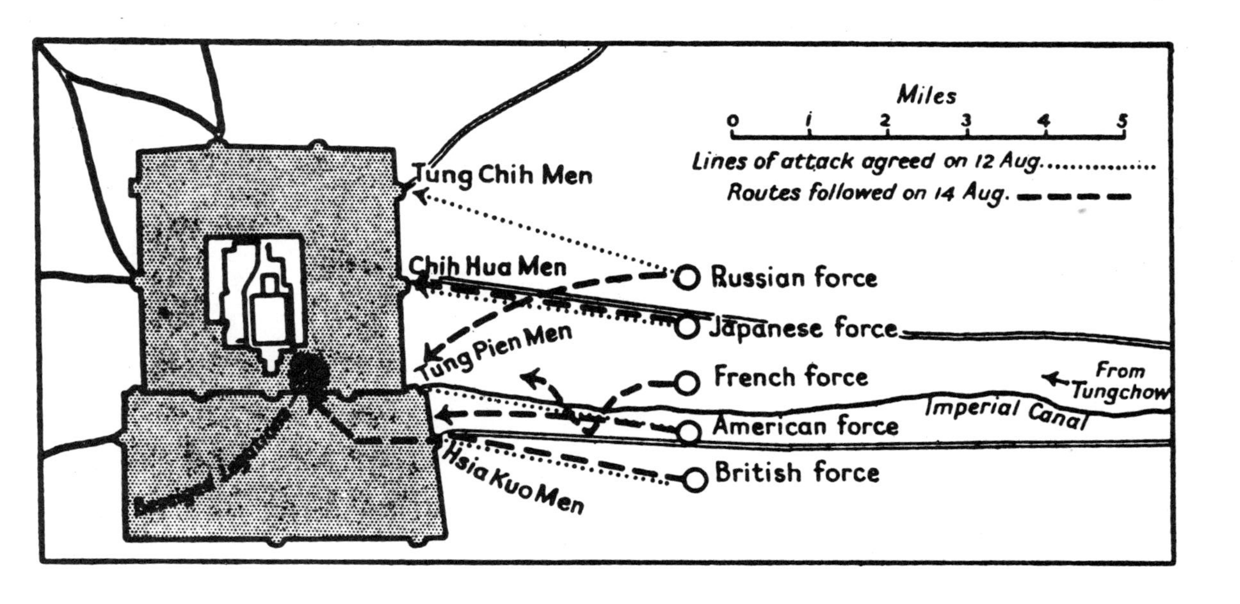

Diagram of the final allied assault on Peking.

after the troops arrived. The Chinese retreated west, on the road that runs past the south gate of the Imperial Palace by the Five Marble Bridges.

The American troops came to Peking on the right of the British. They advanced along the south bank of the Tungchou-Peking canal, and attacked the Tungpienmen, the northeast gate of the Chinese city. They encountered a very strong Chinese resistance there, passed through a Russian unit that was holed up and waiting for reinforcement, and broke through the gate. When they got inside the Tungpienmen, however, they discovered that their route to the legation quarter was flanked all the way by the Tartar wall and they would have to clear the Chinese snipers from the wall, foot by foot, so they could advance. They moved a street away from the wall, and then up to the Hatamen gate and into the legation quarter by the water gate.

Those Russians through whom they moved had a heroic story to tell. These were the advance party of the Russians who had advanced so bravely but so foolishly right up to the gates of Peking on the day before and had called for reinforcements. Late on the night of August 13 they had gone quietly to the point at the outer walls of the city where the Chinese and Tartar cities joined. They had only three guns with them and an escort of 400 infantrymen. They killed the Chinese guards on duty on the bridge and then began firing on the Tungpienmen, blowing a hole in it. Then they moved along the Tartar wall.

Suddenly the moon arose and exposed them fully to the enemy. The Chinese began firing and killed nearly all the horses of the gun battery. The soldiers had to pull the guns back into shelter, about a half-mile away. Twenty-six men

The southern wall of the Tartar City. This picture gives some idea of the vastness of the defenses of Peking.

were killed and 102 were wounded that night, and that is why the Russian force could not move on without supplies and reinforcements.

The Japanese attacked against the Tongchimen and the Tsaihunmen of the Tartar city, having come up the Tungchou road. Intelligence reports had told the Japanese that the Russians were already inside the city, so they marched up to the gates in columns, expecting no resistance. Suddenly, when the Japanese came within rifle range, Chinese troops on the wall began firing at them. The Japanese immediately broke ranks and slid into houses and other shelters on the sides of the roadway. A regiment of infantry was sent in advance, followed by Japanese engineers, who were detailed to blow open the gate after the infantry cleared the way. But the Chinese fire was too heavy. In a few minutes sixteen Japanese were killed or wounded, and the advancing party had to draw back.

The Japanese guns were brought up to a point 1,200 yards behind the city wall and a continuous fire of artillery was begun and maintained by eighteen field guns and thirty-six mountain guns.

Against the walls of the Tartar City, even that many guns did not produce much result, for those walls were made of double thicknesses of brick wall, with the intervening space filled with mud and rubble. The guns would have to be trained on the gate itself. That gate was extremely strong, formed by the building of a tunnel beneath the wall, and closed by massive doors, one on the inside and one on the outside. The gate was crowned by a high tower, from which snipers could shoot at the troops. From the standpoint of the attackers the most difficult matter was that the main gate was surrounded by a semicircular wall, whose enclosure was entered by another gate placed at right angles to the main gate. Obviously, it would be no easy task to dislodge the enemy here or crash through his defenses.

Fortunately for the Japanese, the Chinese behind the wall were unable to reply to the field and mountain guns with cannon of their own. They possessed the guns all right — nine modern Krupps guns and a hundred old-fashioned guns were in place — but in bombarding the legations for a two-month period, the guns had exhausted their ammunition. So the Japanese artillerymen had it all their own way.

During the day the Japanese fired more than 4,500 shells at wall and gate, doing almost no damage to the wall but killing a number of Chinese behind it. Later, about 300 dead Chinese troops and Boxers would be found behind this section of the wall. Japanese losses were high, however, and before nightfall the Japanese command reported about 200 dead and wounded men.

The guns roared long after midnight. Finally, by the light of a brilliant moon, the Japanese troops launched an attack against the gate and crashed their way through, then fought through the streets until morning, when they reached the legations.

On that night of August 14 the people inside the legations slept soundly for the first time in months. The troops of the 7th Rajputs relieved the legation guards, and the Chinese attackers were quieter than they had been in many days. They were still active, however, as the 7th Rajputs discovered.

The British forces cut a hole through the wall of the Imperial Carriage Park, which formed the western boundary of the British legation. It had been the custom of the Chinese Boxers and Imperial troops to occupy the park in the daylight hours and harry the legations with rifle fire. The morning of August 15 was to be no exception, it seemed, for the Chinese moved with the dawn to their barricades. But this time the British were waiting for them in force and as the Chinese moved in they were mowed down like wheat. Later in the morning the British troops occupied the carriage park and cleared it of all Chinese. They then began the laborious process of clearing the adjoining Chinese houses of men with guns.

The Su Wang Fu area after the siege.

The gate of the Forbidden City, Peking.

Fighting continued on August 15, all day long, largely in the western part of the city, where the Americans were attacking the Winter Palace. The Forbidden City now became the scene of the battle, too, because the Chinese troops took refuge there. The Americans had entered by the Tung Pien gate and then attacked the Chinese.

For five days the Imperial Court had been planning to flee west to Sian, onetime capital of one of the ancient Three Kingdoms of China, and the officials of the west were alerted to prepare the Sian Palace for the Dowager Empress and the Emperor. On August 10 the Dowager Empress decreed that Jung Lu, Hsu T'ung, Kang I and Chung I remain in Peking to take charge of government affairs, while the court left for the west. Two days later Li Hung-chang, one of the most trusted of Chinese diplomats and officials, sent a Memorial to the Dowager Empress, advising against leaving the city. The Memorial did not reach the old woman, and she and the court fled. On August 15, as the smoke of battle still hung above Peking, Their Majesties put on simple clothes and the retinue set out for the west. There was no time to make Imperial carts ready, and the British were in the process of taking over the Imperial Carriage Park, so the Dowager Empress rode in the cart of Duke Lan, while the Emperor rode in the cart of Ying Nien, commander of the Peking military force. The Empress and the Heir Apparent were forced to ride in the cart of a commoner.

Only eight officials went west with the Dowager Empress and her retinue. They went out by way of the northwest gate, farthest from the attacking Westerners, and stopped for a brief rest at the Summer Palace outside the city. They rode on for twenty miles more that day, west to Kuanshih, where they stayed overnight in a temple. Two days later the party arrived at Huailai, where they stayed for three days.

Meanwhile, in Peking, during the afternoon of August 16, the French troops and a large force of Japanese circled around the Forbidden City and relieved the

Pehtang, the Roman Catholic Mission where about fifty French and Italian priests and a handful of Italian marines had been under siege for two months. The siege of the mission was conducted even more fiercely than that of the legations, for while after the fall of Peking 92 shell holes were counted in the Hotel de Pekin, in one day alone 300 shells were fired at the mission, where more than 3,000 Chinese Christians had taken refuge from the Boxers who would murder them on sight.

Other troops took possession of the Meshan, or Coal Hill, which was the highest spot in Peking, overlooking the Forbidden City and the Tombs of the Manchus. Only the Forbidden City was still not entered by the foreigners. No foreigner had ever entered parts of this city.

The departure of the Imperial Court for the west made it impossible for any Chinese government officials to begin treating with the foreigners. Earlier, the Tsungli Yamen had informed its embassies abroad that the Chinese Empire wished peace. The Americans and others had suggested that Chinese representatives meet the foreign column of troops outside the city and begin negotiations for peace. The Dowager Empress never heard of this plan, and it is doubtful that she would have accepted it, for until the last she was inclined to follow the advice of the reactionaries who had brought Li Ping-heng to power and changed the course of the Boxer Rebellion.

Li Hung-chang wanted to avoid what must now certainly come about, given the odd mixture of foreign troops in Peking, the confusions that reigned in the departure of the legitimate government and the greed of soldiers in their sacking and looting of Peking.

This looting was one of the sorriest stories to come out

Several of the towers on the wall of the Forbidden City, Peking.

of China in modern history. It began on the morning of August 16. Lieutenant Colonel Vaughan of the 7th Rajputs described what he saw:

> On the 16th we went out into the city, and found the foreign troops hard at work looting; men straggling about in every direction with boxes, furs and ornaments. Parties were sent out under command of officers

with orders to bring in what they could find to the Prize Committee, which was now started. One of these found a mandarin's house, and the store of wine and tinned provision in it formed a welcome addition to the commissariat rations we had been living on for so long. Large quantities of furs and silks were also found, which went to the Prize Committee. Looting on the part of the British troops was carried on in *the most orderly manner* [italics are the author's] and the houses of all those known to be friendly were protected.

It should be remembered that it is one of the unwritten laws of war that a city which does not surrender at the last and is taken by storm is looted. Numberless instances could be quoted, and considering the cowardly and unprovoked attack on the legations, and the murder of Europeans, including helpless women and children, under circumstances of the most revolting cruelty, the Chinese were treated by us far better than they deserved. Many reports were current that the troops of other Powers, one in particular [he meant Russian] shot every person they saw, armed or unarmed, whether man, woman or child; but no instance of this ever came under my observation, beyond the fact that corpses of unarmed peasantry were seen lying about.

Lieutenant Colonel Vaughan did not see very much. Others saw far more in the disgraceful first days of occupation of the fallen city. Bertram Lenox Simpson, who had undergone the siege of the legations, later wrote an eyewitness account of the siege and the rape of Peking. He awoke early, he said, on the morning of August 16. He wrote:

Day had not broken properly before the murmur and movements of the night before rose again . . . There were bugle calls and trumpet calls, the neighing and whinnying of horses, the rumble of heavy wagons, calls and cries . . . But hidden by the high walls and the barricades, nothing could be seen. We got something to eat, and wishing to explore, I marched down to the dry canal bed, jumped in, and made for the water gate, through which the first men had come. In a few steps I was outside the Tartar wall, for the first time for nearly three long months. At last there was something to be seen. Far along here, there were nothing but bivouacs of soldiery moving uneasily like ants suddenly disturbed, and as I tramped through the sand towards the great Chien Men gate I could see columns of other men already in movement, although day had just come, winding in and out from the outer Chinese city. Thick pillars of smoke that hung dully in the morning air were rising in the distance as if fire had been set to many buildings, but apart from these marching troops there was not a living soul to be seen. Thus ruins and the houses had become mere landmarks and the city a veritable desert.

Simpson made his way to the gates of the Imperial Palace in idle curiosity.

I thought, with my mouth watering a little, although I had no actual desire for riches, of General Montauban, created Comte de Palikao, because in the 1860 expedition, when the famous Summer Palace was so ruthlessly sacked, he had taken all the most splendid black pearls he could find and had carried them back to the Empress

Eugenie as a little offering. If one could only get past this boundary and the protocol had not stepped in!

(Actually the Forbidden City was not entered that day, nor for another nine days. The Chinese guards kept the foreigners out of this most sacred of places.)

Simpson saw soldiers looting everywhere. He came to a Chinese guardhouse, one of the dozens that lined the walls of the palace, and there joined a number of American troops in making a gruesome discovery:

> Grovelling on the ground lay an elderly Chinese whose peculiar aspect and general demeanor made it clear what he was. He was a palace eunuch, left here by some strange luck. The man was in a paroxysm of fear, and pointing into the guardhouse behind him he was beseeching the soldiery with words and gestures not to treat him as those inside had been handled. Through the open door I could see a confused mass of dead bodies — men who had been bayonetted to death in the early morning — and from a rafter hung a miserable wretch, who had destroyed himself in his agony to escape the terror of cold steel. As the details became clear, the scene was hideous. Never, indeed, shall I forget that horrid little vignette of war — those dozens upon dozens of curious soldier faces framed in slouch hats only half understanding; the imploring eunuch on the ground, the huddled mass of slaughtered men swimming in their blood in the shadow behind; that thick smell of murder and sudden death rising and stinking in the hot air; and the last cruel note of that Chinese figure, with a shriek of agony and fear petrified on the features, swinging in long, loose clothes from the rafter

> above. In the bright sunlight and the sudden silence which had come over everything, there was a peculiar menace in all this which chilled one. . . .

Simpson watched the killing and the looting all that day, and at the end of the day he came upon a scene that typified everything that was happening in Peking on August 16, 1900:

> That evening as dusk fell, and I was idly watching some English sappers [engineers] blowing an entrance from the canal street through the Pink Palace walls, so that a private right of way into this precious area could be had right where the twin cannon were fired at us for so many weeks, a sound of a rude French song being chanted made me turn around. I saw then that it was a soldier of the Infanterie Coloniale [French] in his faded blue suit of Nankeen, staggering along with his rifle slung across his back and a big gunny sack on his shoulder. He approached, singing lustily in a drunken sort of way, and reeling more and more, until, as he tried to step over the ruins of a brick barricade, he at last tripped and fell heavily to the ground. The English sappers watched him curiously for a few moments as he lay moving drunkenly on the ground, unable to rise, but no one offered to help him, or even stepped forward until one soldier, who had been looking fixedly at something on the ground, said suddenly to his mates in a hoarse whisper, "Silver! Silver!" He spoke in an extraordinary way.
>
> I stepped forward at these words to see. It was true. The sack had been split open by the fall, and on the ground now scattered about lay big half-moons of silver

> – *sycee,* as it is called. The sappers took a cautious look around, saw that all was quiet and only myself there; and then the six of them, seized with the same idea, went quietly forward and plundered the fallen Frenchman of his loot as he lay. Each man stuffed as many of those lumps as he could carry into his shirt or tunic. Then they helped the fallen drunkard to his feet, handed him the fraction of his treasure which remained, and pushed him roughly away. The last I noticed of this curious scene was this marauder staggering into the night, and calling faintly at intervals, as he realized his loss, "*Sacrés voleurs! Sacrés voleurs anglais!*" [Damned robbers! Damned English robbers!] Then I made off too. It was the first open looting I had seen. I shall always remember absolutely how curiously it impressed me. It seemed very strange.

The looting continued for days, and while later the various foreign commanders each tried to blame the others, every nation was involved in it. They broke into warehouses filled with priceless furs and silks, and trampled them to the ground in their eagerness to steal. They looked for gold and jewels, taking the pins out of the hair of the Chinese women, murdering any who resisted, piling up huge heaps of loot, losing it to other looters and going out to loot again.

In these few days of looting nearly all of the province of Chihli was devastated. The villages along the line of march of the foreign troops were entirely destroyed. Most of Peking was burned or pillaged and a third of Tientsin was destroyed. Tungchou, a walled city of 80,000 people, was nearly all destroyed. Scarcely a house was left standing in Chang Chia-wan, a town of 10,000 people. In those first few days the living were driven away to seek food and lodging where they might. The allied troops could not be bothered with the people or with discipline.

By August 18 some semblance of order was returning to the military forces in Peking. During the three days past they had run wild, but now came a systematic reorganization, for although most of the Chinese troops and Boxers had fled, some remained, and street fighting continued in Peking.

On August 18 a force of Bengal Lancers and the 7th Rajputs left the south gate of Peking, accompanied by artillerymen and their batteries to clear out enemy forces nearby. Their immediate destination was the Imperial hunting park where a number of Boxers had holed up.

On reaching the wall of the hunting park, the troops marched through the gate and about 500 yards inside. The cavalry was then deployed to scout. Almost immediately the cavalrymen were attacked by a dozen Boxers. The cavalrymen swung their sabres and killed half a dozen Boxers. The rest then fled back about 800 yards where a large body of Boxers had gathered. The cavalry moved away from the front line, and the field artillery went into action, with the infantrymen firing their rifles at the Boxers. The Boxer force, estimated to be about 1,000 men, retreated over the hill. The British then advanced to a village which had been occupied by the Boxers, burned it, then returned to Peking.

While the foreigners sacked Peking, the Chinese troops retreated west, looting the towns and villages through which they passed, because their supply lines and discipline had broken down. Each man took what he could find

The 1st Bengal Lancers leaving Peking.

to eat, to wear and to enrich himself. The Imperial Court designated several of the most prominent generals to stop the pillaging by Chinese soldiers along the retreat line. General Tung Fu-hsiang was ordered to guard the border between Chihli and Shansi against foreign troops and looters. The old diplomat, Li Hung-chang, was also ordered to make every effort to establish relations with the foreign governments and bring about peace. Then the Imperial Court continued its move westward toward Sian in Shensi province, a trip that would take a month.

Li Hung-chang, the man who was now given power to resolve the war in behalf of the Imperial Throne, was the leading statesman of China. In 1870 he had been appointed Viceroy of Chihli and for twenty-five years he had been the most important official in the Chinese government. In 1895, after the defeat in the Sino-Japanese war, he had been dismissed as Viceroy of Chihli, and made the scapegoat of the defeat. He had then gone on to become Viceroy of Kwangtung and Kwangsi and had moved to far-off Canton.

In June, when the diplomatic situation had become serious, the old Dowager Empress had ordered Li Hung-chang to come to Peking. Li had begun to do so, ordering a ship to bring him from Canton to Taku, but as the situation worsened, he delayed, probably remembering that he had once been the goat for a lost war, and not wanting to be involved. In July he was reappointed Viceroy of Chihli, and again ordered north, and this time he sailed from Canton to Shanghai, arriving there July 21.

In Shanghai, friends persuaded Li Hung-chang to remain, not to go on to Peking, and General Yuan Shih-kai informed him by telegram that the reactionaries were in control and had persuaded the Dowager Empress to make war on the foreigners. So Li remained in Shanghai, safe

Li Hung-chang, the viceroy who negotiated with the foreign powers on behalf of the Imperial Throne.

from the reactionary ministers who were in control, and sent messages to the Dowager Empress asking that the Boxers be suppressed and the foreign diplomats be saved.

One of the confusing aspects of the Boxer Rebellion is that two policies were being pursued by the Chinese at the same time. All the southern governors wanted peace and the suppression of the Boxers. They so informed the foreigners and they agitated for peace through their messages to Peking. On the one hand, the Dowager Empress indicated that she was paying attention to their demands and on the other she paid attention to the reactionaries around her who wanted war.

Li Hung-chang became so upset about the execution of the five liberal ministers that he asked for sick leave – a polite way of telling the Dowager Empress that he disapproved of her policy and did not want to represent her. She refused his request on August 7 and appointed him plenipotentiary minister, with power to negotiate with the foreign powers on behalf of the Imperial Throne.

When Peking fell, and the court fled, there was only one man who could bring an end to the war and prevent what the wise men knew was about to happen: the partition of China into colonies of the foreign governments. Li Hung-chang was ordered to begin negotiations with the foreigners, but still he delayed. And in Shanghai, where a number of important foreigners had come, the British and the Germans indicated that they did not wish to negotiate with Li. So the problem remained unsolved for many weary days.

On August 28, as Li Hung-chang continued his maneuverings in Shanghai, the full force of the Chinese defeat was brought home. On that day, for the first time in history, foreigners marched through the gates and invaded the sacred soil of the Forbidden City. The Russians led the parade and the Japanese came second. The British were third and the Americans followed them.

The foreign troops continued mopping-up operations against the Boxers in and around Peking, but the war was far from over. The foreigners controlled Peking, the capital, but the government had moved far to the west. The foreigners controlled a line of communications that ran to Tientsin and the sea, but the Boxers still controlled the countryside of Chihli and all the other northern provinces.

For two months the foreigners argued among themselves, their governments at home quite at odds as to how the China problem should be settled. At the end of August, the Russians in St. Petersburg suggested that the foreigners should withdraw their armies from Peking, since they had gone there to rescue the foreign legation officials and their families and this task had been accomplished. The Russians said the foreign troops should all return to Tientsin. Only when the Chinese Imperial government returned to Peking from the west could a peace settlement be made. It was the Russians' idea that this return should be speeded as quickly as possible. To show their good faith, the Russians sent their minister to Tientsin. But when only the French agreed with this view, it failed to carry among the foreigners, and the Russian minister finally came back to Peking.

Li Hung-chang went to Tientsin aboard a Chinese ship on September 16, 1900. Now he was to begin the peace negotiations that would determine the fate of the Dowager Empress and her court. Finally, after much hemming and hawing, he had been given complete power by the Dowager Empress to carry out negotiations with the foreigners. The skill of this seventy-seven-year-old diplomat was to be tested in Tientsin.

10 | NEGOTIATIONS FOR PEACE

When Li Hung-chang arrived in Tientsin he was forced into working closely with the Russians for the settlement of the war because the other powers would not deal directly with him. His first act was to petition the Imperial Throne to return to Peking so that negotiations could begin for the peace treaty.

The Dowager Empress refused to return to Peking. In the first place, she said, Peking was now divided by the foreigners into occupation sectors, with each army taking a part of the city and preserving order there. Under such circumstances, neither the common people nor the Chinese government would have any freedom of movement between the sectors. The Dowager Empress had another reason for not wanting to return. She suspected that if she came back the foreigners might force unacceptable demands upon her, and if she refused to accept them they might seize the Imperial family. (One very real fear of the Dowager Empress was that the foreign envoys would demand the return of power to the Emperor. She had never learned that the famous "Demand of Four Points," which her ministers reported to her had been fabricated by the reactionaries around her.)

So the Dowager Empress refused the demand that she return, saying that if the foreign diplomats really wanted peace they would not make such demands. She did promise that as soon as peace was made the court would return to Peking.

The Dowager Empress was now very much under the control of the reactionaries who had caused all the trouble in the beginning. Prince Tuan, one of the major supporters of the Boxers, was a Grand Councillor to the court, and all but one of the Grand Councillors were foreigner-haters who had supported the Boxer movement.

Their plan was to make Sian the headquarters of the Empire and to carry on the war from there. Kang I, one of the leaders of this movement, proposed that the forces of Tung Fu-hsiang and three other generals be increased, and that they be sent to defend T'ungkuan, and later to attack the foreigners, if necessary. The only reason for the defeat of the Chinese by the foreigners, he claimed, was that the Chinese Imperial armies had not been ready for war.

Li Hung-chang and his advisers wanted several of the western and southern viceroys to go to the capital and join the Grand Council, hoping that these men would be able to persuade the Dowager Empress against such foolish plans. But none of the viceroys was willing to go, for the Dowager Empress might very well cut off their heads if they displeased her.

One person so asked was Chang Chih-tung, a longtime official who was then serving as viceroy at Hankow. Chang became very flustered when he was asked to go to Sian. His health was terrible, he said, and it was getting worse. He slept no more than two-and-a-half hours each day. His mind was clear for only about four hours a day, he added. He could not even read the papers any more, because reading made him dizzy. His legs were too weak to walk, and he could not stand a journey by sea. He begged, "with thousands of kowtows," to be excused from the duty.

Finally Jung Lu was persuaded to join the Grand Council. He was eager to do so, for an entirely different reason. Jung Lu had done his best to prevent the war, in his own devious way, but the foreign diplomats did not know that fact, and they disliked Jung Lu and held him to be one of their enemies because his troops had been among those surrounding the legation quarter. Jung Lu had been chosen by the Dowager Empress to join Li Hung-chang in the negotiations with the foreigners, and Jung Lu had no desire to put himself in a position where he might be imprisoned by the foreigners. So it was arranged that Jung Lu would go to Sian to join the court, and there would represent the moderate view. Dangerous as the assignment might be, it did not seem as dangerous to him as travelling to Tientsin under the circumstances.

By the time Jung Lu arrived at Sian in November, matters had changed there, too. The Dowager Empress had come to realize that the pro-Boxer faction in her council had caused a lot of trouble, and all the council had been dismissed except Wang Wan-shao, Jung Lu and Lu Ch'uan-lin. Wang was a liberal and Jung was a liberal. Lu had been one of those advocating a fight with the British if they tried to send a warship up the Pei Ho, as they talked of doing at one time before the hostilities actually had begun.

The Dowager Empress now seemed to realize that she had been misguided, and she relented in her policy toward the Emperor and toward her ministers. For the first time, the way was clear for real peace negotiations.

The Westerners now decided that before peace negotiations could be carried out, the pro-Boxer ministers who had caused all the trouble must be punished by the Imperial Throne. Chang Chih-tung suggested that this being the case, General Tung Fu-hsiang be sacrificed and all blame be laid on him for the Boxer Rebellion and the use of Imperial troops against the foreigners.

Li Hung-chang knew that the foreigners would not be satisfied with the punishment of only one man, so he suggested that Kang I be punished also. Others added the name of Prince Tuan to the list. Eventually Li suggested to the Dowager Empress that Prince Chuang, Kang I and Ying Nien be punished because they were the three most important Boxer leaders. He added the name of Prince Tuan, who had been the chief patron of the Boxers, and the name of Chao Shu-ch'iao, who had pretended to investigate the Boxers and had reported that they were not dangerous to China.

Li suggested that after the Imperial Throne had punished these men, negotiations could begin.

The old Empress then acted. She deprived Prince Chuang and two other princes of their titles of nobility. She did the same with Prince Tuan but handed him over to the Clansmen's Court, a special court to try nobles, for further action. Ying Nien, Kang I, Chao Shu-ch'iao and several others were also recommended for punishment.

But these punishments, while very serious in Chinese eyes because they ruined the lives of the men and their families, were not serious enough for the allies. They wanted blood. On October 30, Li Hung-chang reported that the foreigners insisted on the execution of nine princes and ministers, as well as of Tung Fu-hsiang and Yu Hsien. Li suggested that this be done immediately so the negotiations could continue.

The Dowager Empress would not do it. She said Tung Fu-hsiang was a soldier who had done as he was told. She said that she would exile Yu Hsien, the old governor of Shantung who had encouraged the Boxer Rebellion in the beginning.

Jung Lu interceded for heavy punishment. So the punishments were made heavier, except against Kang I, who had died by this time from an illness. Prince Tuan and Prince Chuang were to be imprisoned for life at Mukden. Yu Hsien was to be banished to the western frontier and forced to serve at hard labor for the rest of his life. Others were to be imprisoned or degraded in rank. General Tung Fu-hsiang's punishment was to be considered later, because he had been acting as a soldier, under orders.

The foreigners were not satisfied yet, for they wanted the punishment of Tung Fu-hsiang. This attitude created some serious problems for the court because Tung Fu-hsiang was very popular with the people of Kansu and Shensi. He was a Kansu man, and his Moslem troops appealed to the heavily Moslem populations of these two provinces. His troops were stationed at Sian, 15,000 of them, and there were no other strong forces in the area.

The foreigners had among themselves many different points of view. The Russians were pursuing their ambition of controlling Manchuria, and they were trying to achieve concessions from the Chinese government, so they advocated a soft policy toward China. The Germans had suffered the murder of their Baron von Ketteler, and for this and reasons of their own they wanted a very harsh policy. The Kaiser wished to expand his influence in the Far East and the Germans had their eyes on more territory. A German, Field Marshal von Waldersee, was finally appointed commander-in-chief of the allied forces and he wished to continue to prosecute the war against the Chinese. The allies, were, in fact, moving troops west toward Sian all during the negotiations.

The British, who were afraid of Russian influence in China, sided with the Germans. The Japanese were also worried about the Russians, but they adopted a conciliatory line and said they would negotiate without punishments of officials or return of the court to Peking — although other foreigners were holding out for these conditions.

The French talked with the Russians, but voted with the Germans and the English in the meetings of the foreign powers in China. The Americans stood for moderation. They rejected the German demand that the allies punish the Chinese ministers who had encouraged the Boxers and the war. Secretary of State John Hay adopted a policy toward China that was to be known later as the Open Door Policy. The idea was to encourage the buildup of trade between China and all nations of the world, without taking more territory away from China or causing her more pain.

In December, 1900, after considerable negotiation and consideration, the foreigners submitted a document containing twelve demands. China was to express regrets about the murder of Baron von Ketteler and erect a monument to his memory. All those persons named by the court as responsible for the rebellion should be punished. Japan must be recompensed for the murder of Mr. Sugiyama, chancellor of the Japanese legation and monuments must be erected in the cemeteries that had been desecrated by the Boxers. China could produce no more arms. Indemnities must be paid. The foreigners should have the right to keep guards in the legation area. No Chinese could live in the legation quarter. The Taku forts would be destroyed. The foreigners were to be able to guard lines of communication to the sea. It must be made illegal to belong to an anti-foreign society, and an offense punishable by death. New treaties must be negotiated with the foreign powers. The Chinese government must reform the Tsungli Yamen.

These were harsh terms and some members of the Grand Council objected to them. The Imperial Court – meaning the Dowager Empress – was inclined to object, too, but Li Hung-chang pointed out that the foreigners had no intention of discussing their demands. If the court argued the matter, the negotiations would be suspended and the foreigners would prosecute the war against China. He suggested that they might capture Sian and the Imperial Court itself.

Such argument was effective. On January 10 the Dowager Empress ordered that the twelve articles be signed and four days later it was done.

Officially, the Boxer Rebellion was over. But there were many problems still to be solved.

11 | CHINA AND THE SETTLEMENT

While the Russians talked like friends of China, during the Boxer Rebellion they had occupied the three provinces of Manchuria, after subduing Chinese troops in battle. They took the cities of Tsitsihar, Harbin, Mukden and Liaoyang. They settled down then to occupy this portion of China and make it their own.

Japan objected very strenuously to this move by Russia, and in the negotiations that followed the Russians were forced to give way. They agreed that they would return the three provinces to Chinese control, but they indicated that it would take considerable time to do so, because the railroads that the Russians now controlled must be protected. In the autumn, as negotiations were going on in Peking, the Chinese generals in the three provinces of Kirin, Feng-t'ien and Heilungkiang began negotiating with the Russians for the return of the Chinese territory. Tartar General Tseng Ch'i had already begun negotiating even as the Chinese throne so advised him.

Tseng Ch'i was negotiating with Admiral Evgenyi Ivanovitch Alexeieff, the governor of the Liaotung peninsula, who was the viceroy of the Tsar in East Asia. An agreement was reached toward the end of the year. The Imperial Court did not like the agreement when it was finally called to the court's attention, but there was nothing to be done about it because the Russians insisted on having it.

The Dowager Empress was in no position to protest. This agreement was important to the Russians because it gave them a legal basis for continued occupation of Manchuria, and they had no intention of returning the territory without being sure that they profited from its capture. In January, 1901, the Russians began negotiating with Yang Ju, the Chinese minister to Russia, for the return of all three Manchurian provinces. The Russians insisted that the negotiations be carried out in St. Petersburg, and the Chinese could again do nothing but accept the demand.

Having first seized the territory, the Russians had seen that there was too much objection from Japan and other powers. Now they proposed to return the land to China, but they wanted to be sure that no other powers were allowed in, and that foreign capital, other than Russian, was kept out. What the Russians proposed to do, and Yang Ju commented on it, was to establish a protectorate, of the kind that Britain had over India. Yang Ju transmitted Thirteen Points that the Russians wanted, but he also told the Chinese government that if the points were accepted China would lose the power of defending Manchuria, of deciding on industrial development and of appointing officials to rule the land. The Russians would, in effect, gain all those powers over Chinese territory. Further, the agreement was to include not only Manchuria, but Mongolia. He suggested that if the Imperial Court accepted this agreement, the other powers would proceed to chop China up into a series of colonies. Germany might take all of Shantung province. Britain might take the Yangtze valley. France would take Kwangsi in the south. What would Japan want? What would other countries want? What would be left?

When the Thirteen Points reached Peking and Li Hung-chang, he agreed with the minister, and when they reached the Dowager Empress she, too, agreed, and so the negotiations with Russia were deferred by her orders.

Furthermore, the Japanese became very upset. At this time Russia and Japan were competing for dominance in the Far East. Russia wanted the warmwater ports of Korea open for her use. Japan wanted power over Korea. Russia and Japan had agreed to discuss the question of Korea, but now the Japanese said that they wanted to wait until the Manchurian question was settled before talking any further about Korea.

The Russians finally saw that they were creating endless difficulties for themselves by their insistence that Manchuria be turned over to them. They agreed to forget the Tseng-Alexeieff agreement. Finally their terms were considerably softened, but they still demanded immense power, and the Chinese government was not willing to grant it. The negotiations lasted for months. By July, 1901, the other powers were taking a hand and Britain and Japan were doing all they could to cut down Russian influence. Japan in particular was annoyed because after the Sino-Japanese War Japan had won agreement that she was to have control of the Liaotung peninsula, where Port Arthur is located, and pressure had been brought on her to evacuate the territory. Under separate agreements, the Russians had gained control of Port Arthur and the peninsula, and now the Russians were trying to take control of all Manchuria and Mongolia.

Meanwhile, the Chinese court was negotiating with all the foreign powers about settlement of the claims that arose out of the Boxer Rebellion. There was much argument about the punishment to be given the principal offenders. Finally, on February 13, the Dowager Empress issued a decree. Of her advisers, Prince Chuang was to commit suicide. Prince Tuan and Duke Lan were banished to Sinkiang province in the far and lonely west, for the rest of their lives, and were imprisoned there. Yu Hsien was executed. Ying Nien and Chao Shu-ch'iao were ordered to commit suicide. Tung Fu-hsiang was deprived of his command and his honors. Kang I, Hsu T'ung, and Li Ping-heng were all deprived of honors, even in death. Ch'i Hsiu and Hsu Cheng-yu were executed, and, finally, 119 other persons on lower levels were penalized, to degrees ranging from execution to reprimand.

The foreigners, with the exception of the Americans, were determined to exact all they could from China. According to the French, the United States did all it could to keep China from being punished. Minister Conger began by trying to keep the amount of the reparations payment down. The other nations demanded 450,000,000 taels, or £67,000,000, a staggering sum that China could not afford to pay. Eventually, that is what China had to pay because the Germans and Russians held out for so much. In order to make the payments, the Chinese had to pledge their import revenues, and the foreigners thus cemented control of the Chinese customs services.

Finally, with all these agreements, on September 7, 1901, almost thirteen months after the allies had marched into Peking, the peace treaty was signed by the foreign nations and the Chinese representatives of the Dowager Empress. On October 6 the Imperial Court began its journey back to Peking, and on January 7, 1902, the Dowager Empress, the Emperor, the Empress, the Heir Apparent, and all the courtiers returned to the Forbidden City. In April the Russians finally agreed to evacuate Manchuria within the next eighteen months. Peace seemed to have been returned to the Far East.

12 | RESULTS OF THE REBELLION

The Boxer Rebellion represented anti-foreign sentiment in China, and this sentiment was not stamped out by the Imperial Throne's decree that it was against the law to belong to an anti-foreign society. Anti-foreign sentiment simply went underground in China, to remain underground for forty years.

"Anti-foreign" in this sense was a purely Chinese concept, and in more modern terms it would be called anti-imperialist, but in 1900 imperialism was not an evil word in the world. All the Western powers supported imperialism, and even the United States under the McKinley and Theodore Roosevelt administrations, dabbled in imperialism.

Until World War II began the Boxer movement was the last fight of the Chinese people to keep their independence. Later Sun Yat-sen was to try to build a modern China and Chiang Kai-shek was to resist Japanese imperialism, but the imperialism of the West by this time was too deeply rooted to be wiped out by anything less than a major explosion in China. Western foreign influence was not eliminated from China until the Communists seized control of the Chinese government in 1949.

The Russians lost most of their influence in China three years after the signing of the treaty that ended the Boxer Rebellion. Because of the course Russia followed, it was inevitable that a struggle would take place between the Tsar's government and Japan. After the Russo-Japanese War of 1904-1905, Japan became the dominant power in Manchuria, and seized all the privileges that the Russians had sought.

To understand Russia's interests in 1945, at the Yalta meeting of the heads of state, one must go back to the Boxer Rebellion and historic Russian foreign policy. The fact that the Russian government in 1900 was imperial and the Russian government forty years later was Communist does not seem to have made much difference. The division of Korea at the 38th parallel represented an old Russian policy. And when World War II ended, the Russians moved quickly into Manchuria, dismantling its industry and shipping that industry back to Russia, rather than leaving it for the Chinese. What was left was securely placed in the hands of the Chinese Communists.

The Japanese arms and the control of Manchuria that was thus almost assured to the Chinese Communists became the basis for their eventual victory in the civil war. Then, for a time, Russian influence was very strong in China. But ten years after the Communists won control, they began to become very restless under Russian influence, and the old anti-foreignism or anti-imperialism again raised its head.

Anti-imperialism was always present during the intervening years. During the nineteen-twenties, in the Yangtze valley, students rose up against the foreigners a number of times and for several months they unloaded all the foreign products that were shipped up the river, thus preventing delivery of the goods.

In the foreign settlements in Shanghai, Canton, Tientsin and elsewhere there were often riots against the foreigners. The fact that the riots were suppressed did not mean that they failed to represent a strong and basic Chinese feeling.

For hundreds of years under many dynasties the Chinese had been among the most powerful people of the world. Suddenly, at the turn of the twentieth century, China was reduced to colonial status, and the intelligent Chinese never forgot or forgave this insult and injury.

Certainly not all the developments in China in the twentieth century can be explained in terms of the Boxer Rebellion, but it is equally certain that no one can understand the attitudes of the Chinese, in such matters as the Red Guard movement that sprang up in the nineteen-sixties, unless one knows why and how Chinese sentiment against foreign influences was born.

Bibliography

Headland, Isaac T. *Chinese Heroes*. New York: Eaton and Mains, 1902.

Laur, Francis. *Le Siège de Peking*. Paris: Societé des Publications Scientifiques et Industrielles, 1905.

Li, Dun J. *The Ageless Chinese*. New York: Charles Scribner's Sons, 1965.

Steiger, George Nye. *China and the Occident*. New Haven: Yale University Press, 1927; London: Oxford University Press.

Tan, Chester C. *The Boxer Catastrophe*. New York: Columbia University Press, 1955; London: Oxford University Press.

Thomson, H.C. *China and the Powers*. London: Longmans Green and Co., 1902.

Vaughan, H.B. *St. George and the Chinese Dragon*. London: Arthur Pearson Ltd., 1902.

Weale, L.P. (pseudonym) [L.L. Simpson, ed.] *Indiscreet Letters from Peking*. New York: Dodd, Mead and Co., 1907; London: Hurst and Blackett.

Index

INDEX